Cambridge Grocer
The story of Matthew's of Trinity Street 1832-1962

Judy Wilson, née Matthew, was born in Cambridge and brought up in Caxton, where she went to school before going to the Perse School for Girls in Cambridge. She attended Birmingham and later, Loughborough Universities. Before returning to live in Cambridgeshire, she lived in Africa, Nottingham and London, largely working in local and national health charities. Judy has written three other books, on self help groups and in 2001 was awarded the OBE for services to health care.

D1494578

Cambridge Grocer

The story of
Matthew's of Trinity Street
1832–1962

Judy Wilson

Judy Wilson

First published in 2010 by R A Wilson.

A CIP catalogue record for this book is available from the British Library.

ISBN 978-1-874259-02-2

Designed & typeset by *Moyhill* Graphic Design.

Printed in the UK by Direct-POD, Brixworth, Northampton.

R A Wilson

'Cambridge Grocer',
18 Cambridge Road, Impington, Cambridge CB24 9NU.
Order online at *www.cambridgegrocer.com*

Cambridge Grocer
The story of Matthew's of Trinity Street 1832–1962

Judy Wilson, née Matthew, was born in Cambridge and brought up in Caxton, where she went to school before going to the Perse School for Girls in Cambridge. She attended Birmingham and later, Loughborough Universities. Before returning to live in Cambridgeshire, she lived in Africa, Nottingham and London, largely working in local and national health charities. Judy has written three other books, on self help groups and in 2001 was awarded the OBE for services to health care.

Cambridge Grocer

The story of
Matthew's of Trinity Street
1832–1962

Judy Wilson

First published in 2010 by R A Wilson.

A CIP catalogue record for this book is available
from the British Library.

ISBN 978-1-874259-02-2

Designed & typeset by *Moyhill* Graphic Design.

Printed in the UK
by Direct-POD, Brixworth, Northampton.

The papers used in this book were produced in an
environmentally friendly way from sustainable forests.

R A Wilson

'Cambridge Grocer',
18 Cambridge Road, Impington, Cambridge CB24 9NU.
Order online at *www.cambridgegrocer.com*

To Celia, Richard and Stephen,
my sister and brothers

CONTENTS

MAP SHOWING TRINITY STREET

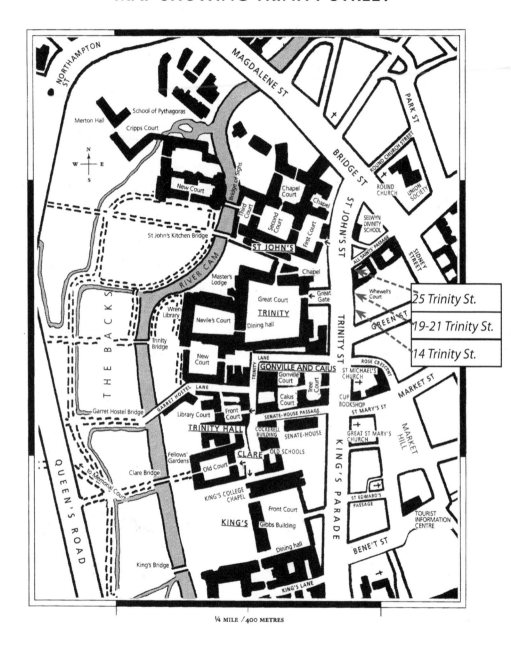

From Marcus Askwith, Kevin Taylor, *Central Cambridge. A Guide to the University and Colleges* 1st edition, © Cambridge University Press 1994

TIMELINE

KEY EVENTS IN THE HISTORY OF
MATTHEW & SON 1829–1962

1829   David Matthew arrives in Cambridge from London, as apprentice to Mr Beechino

1832   David buys a partnership in Browne & Gent and Matthew & Gent opens at 25 Trinity Street, with David as senior partner

1833   John Matthew, David's younger brother, joins him from London

1849   David returns to London while John takes his place as partner with John Gent

1858   The firm moves from 25 Trinity Street to 20–21 Trinity Street, when numbers 24 and 25 were demolished to allow for the building of Whewell's Court by Trinity College

1874   John Matthew and Henry Matthew, John's eldest son, enter into a Deed of Partnership as Matthew & Son

1879   Henry dies suddenly and his wife Margaret takes his place as partner with John, with John's fourth son Arthur returning to Cambridge to work with his father

1884   Arthur Matthew and his father John enter into a Deed of Partnership as Matthew & Son

1889   John dies, leaving the business to Arthur

1894   Lease of 19 Trinity Street, the wine shop, taken on

1895   Matthew & Son becomes a Limited Company, with Arthur as Governing Director

1896   The Café opens at 14 Trinity Street

1917   Arthur dies. His wife Maude becomes Chairman of the Board, Fred Cross is Governing Director, and Arthur's son Bernard spends a year as a trainee in the firm

1919   14 Trinity Street, The Café, purchased from the Foster brothers

1923   Bernard Matthew begins work at Matthew & Son

1937   Bernard becomes Managing Director

1938   14 Trinity Street sold to Trinity College with The Café continuing to trade in the premises, with Matthew & Son becoming Trinity's tenants

1962   Matthew & Son sold to John Harvey & Sons, still trading in Trinity Street as grocers and wine merchants under the Matthew & Son name, but no longer owned by the family

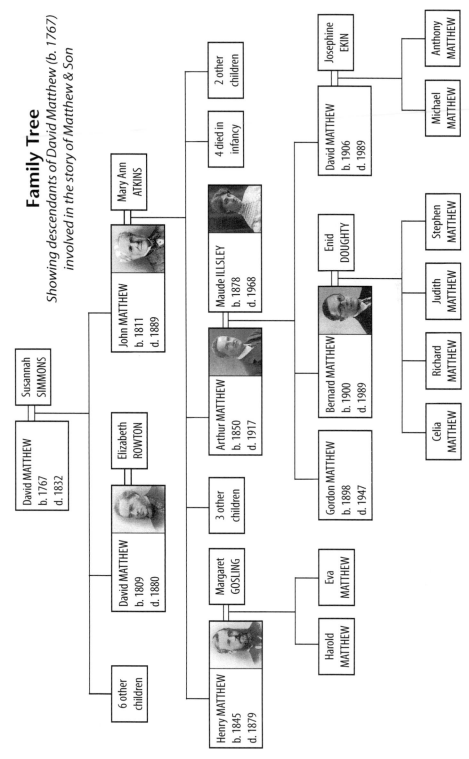

Family Tree

Showing descendants of David Matthew (b. 1767)
involved in the story of Matthew & Son

David MATTHEW
b. 1767
d. 1832

Susannah
SIMMONS

David MATTHEW
b. 1809
d. 1880

Elizabeth
ROWTON

John MATTHEW
b. 1811
d. 1889

Mary Ann
ATKINS

6 other
children

3 other
children

4 died in
infancy

2 other
children

Henry MATTHEW
b. 1845
d. 1879

Margaret
GOSLING

Arthur MATTHEW
b. 1850
d. 1917

Maude ILLSLEY
b. 1878
d. 1968

David MATTHEW
b. 1906
d. 1989

Josephine
EKIN

Harold
MATTHEW

Eva
MATTHEW

Gordon MATTHEW
b. 1898
d. 1947

Bernard MATTHEW
b. 1900
d. 1989

Enid
DOUGHTY

Michael
MATTHEW

Anthony
MATTHEW

Celia
MATTHEW

Richard
MATTHEW

Judith
MATTHEW

Stephen
MATTHEW

1.1 David Matthew, founder of Matthew & Gent, as a young man, 1830s.

1: HOW IT ALL BEGAN – DAVID MATTHEW AND THE EARLY YEARS

The founder of Matthew & Son, David Matthew, was ambitious, capable and entrepreneurial, quickly proving himself to be an astute businessman. David arrived in Cambridge in 1829 at the age of just 20, leaving his home in London where his father was a businessman in the brush trade, to become briefly an assistant to a grocer in Sidney Street, Mr Beechino. The grocery business which David Matthew soon established, later to become Matthew & Son, was to last for 130 years, handed down through three generations of the Matthew family until 1962.

Formation of Matthew & Gent

My great-great uncle David was the third son in his family. His father, also called David, had a long-established family firm, D. Matthew & Sons, Bristle Merchant and Brush Manufacturer, where his two older sons were already partners with their father. Though David had no family in Cambridge he took the opportunity to learn a different trade, to settle in a new town, and to strike out on his own. Mr Beechino – a friend of his father, it is thought – had his shop at 57 Sidney Street, in premises opposite Sussex Street, but David did not stay there long. Within only three years, the energetic young man had left Mr Beechino and bought his first shop. David's father died in 1832, which may well have given him the resources to purchase the business of Mr Ridgeway, a china and glass dealer on Bridge Street. It was a short-lived enterprise, a stepping stone to his partnership with Mr John Gent, for David soon became senior partner in Matthew & Gent, Grocers and Dealers in China and Glass. The firm opened for business at 25 Trinity Street later in 1832. John Gent had previously been in partnership with Moses Browne in the same premises and the new firm took on Browne and Gent's

1.2 25 Trinity Street, with awnings, the first premises of Matthew & Gent from 1832 – 1858. Whewell's Court was built on the site.

customers. David inserted a succession of confident advertisements on the front page of the *Cambridge Chronicle*, informing his friends and customers about his move, finally closing the former Ridgeway's warehouse and selling the last of its contents in the summer of 1833.

Prime site and prestigious customers

25 Trinity Street was opposite Trinity College, the largest and richest of all the colleges, the shop being situated on the corner of All Saints Passage and next to the first All Saints Church. Cambridge was a compact town and half the colleges were within a quarter of a mile of the shop. On a prime site, it was well placed to attract college trade, including orders from their Fellows (senior members of the colleges). Another customer was the Assize Judge, who visited Cambridge twice a year and stayed in his own accommodation in Trinity. His cook had made a regular order from Moses Browne, which was inherited by the new firm. Although their next door neighbour at number 24 was also a grocer, Matthew & Gent quickly became a significant supplier to the colleges and their visitors.

1.3 The Coronation Dinner held on Parker's Piece, June 28th 1838.

Six years later in 1838, Queen Victoria's Coronation on June 28th was marked with major celebrations throughout the country. In Cambridge a coronation dinner was held for 15,000 residents of Cambridge on Parker's Piece, with 100 musicians and vocalists performing in the centre and space for 25,000 spectators. David's business was involved in the splendid occasion. Matthew & Gent supplied 72 lb of mustard and 140 lb of salt, at cost price, and provided 1,400 mustard pots and salt plates, cautiously stating, 'Provided the committee be responsible for breakage or loss'. The firm was by then sufficiently established to be commissioned as one of the suppliers of the vast amount of food consumed.

Cambridge – a sound choice

Apart from the University, Cambridge was then largely a country town of only 20,000 people. When David arrived in 1829, most likely travelling on the stage coach from London, the driver would have had to look out for flocks of sheep being driven along Trumpington Road, only a mile from Great Saint Mary's Church and today's Botanical Garden was just a field. Most trade carried on in the town at the time was connected to the colleges and an aspiring businessman would have seen that the prospect of supplying them alone offered great

3

1.4 Cambridge from the first milestone, 1809.

*1.5 Barges bringing goods up the River Cam –
and competing with punts, 1793.*

opportunities. Cambridge University, founded in the early thirteenth century, still had only Oxford as a competitor. The eighteen Cambridge colleges were extraordinarily wealthy and powerful, owning land and controlling ecclesiastical livings right across England. Their Fellows, required to be celibate, lived in their college, and the University had about 800 undergraduates. But it was an expanding town: at the time David came to live in Cambridge, the population was growing and many more houses were being built.

Grocers needed reliable transport for their goods. There was no railway to Cambridge until 1845 but the river was still an important route, with barges on the River Cam coming from as far afield as King's Lynn. The main business of Matthew & Gent was grocery, china and glass but Matthew's was always known for the wide range of goods they stocked and Matthew & Gent even supplied fishermen, issuing fishing licences and selling fishing tackle. The firm employed between six and eight men.

Local resident

In time David became more than a businessman, as did his successors, for all the other Matthew men who later headed the business also contributed to Cambridge's public life as well as managing the firm. (There is one woman in this story, but Maude played a rather different, though crucial role.) In 1847 David Matthew was elected as a councillor on to a reformed Town Council, a good entrée to the civic life of the town and a chance for contacts with other local businessmen. David had soon married. In 1836, Elizabeth Rowton, stepdaughter of Mr James Peters, Silversmith & Jeweller in the Market Place became his wife. He and Elizabeth lived above the shop on Trinity Street and in time had nine children, six born during their time in Cambridge.

Family succession

Family succession was to prove challenging for the firm in later years, but this time there was a smooth changeover. David's younger brother John also moved to Cambridge from London and worked closely with his brother and his partner for sixteen years. John took over when David returned to London in 1849. For within another seventeen years, David had left Cambridge to return to London to take on the family brush manufacturing business, which separated at this time from the bristle business. His stay in Cambridge, just twenty years, was short compared to the other members of the family who in turn took over, but Matthew & Gent was well established by 1849 and securely in the hands of his successor.

David was an innovator, with the skills and energy that starting up something new or different requires. Many years later his grandson Edmund Matthew, part of the brush making business side of the Matthew family, observed in a letter to his cousin Bernard Matthew:

> The amazing people of those days passed from one job to another quite easily. When I recollect that my Grandfather at the age of 40 with six children suddenly gave up a prosperous business as a grocer in Cambridge and took up that of a Brush Manufacturer in London, about which he knew nothing, it only shows the enterprise that people of that day possessed.

David died in London in 1880, at the age of 71. He had benefited from important family support but his own self confidence and effort were pivotal in setting up what was to be a highly successful business – and in laying firm foundations on which his brother John, and then other members of the family, could build.

1.6   David Matthew in mid life, 1850s.

2.1 *John Matthew, 1870s.*

2: FAMILY SUCCESSION –

MATTHEW & GENT TO MATTHEW & SON

Family succession was important in firms like Matthew's. The aim, ideally, was to ensure a smooth handover from one generation to another as a son or brother – and it nearly always was a man – learnt the trade and in time took over. It gave continuity, financial security, jobs for family members and an air of reliability. Customers of the kind who shopped at Matthew & Son, as it became in 1874, liked the feeling of being served by successive generations of the family. Even over eighty years later people would ask me, 'And is your brother going into the business?' Three generations of the family were to run the firm in due course but managing the succession was not always a simple task.

John – successor to David

A handsome portrait hangs on the wall in my brother's home. It portrays John Matthew, our great grandfather and the second member of the family to run the business. John is painted formally dressed, aged perhaps 50, caught with a calm, competent but slightly solemn gaze. Like his older brother David, John had no former connection to Cambridge. Their father, head of the family London brush making business, had died in 1832 when John was 21. He was the youngest of the four sons, and with his two older brothers in charge of the London business, he had soon followed David to join him and David's partner John Gent a year later to work in Matthew & Gent, Grocers and Dealers in China and Glass.

John lived initially in lodgings with a family in nearby Bridge Street and married Mary Ann Atkins, daughter of William Cooper Atkins of Bridge Street, on June 5th 1844. A splendid waistcoat he wore for his wedding has been passed down the family. By the time of the

2.2 John Matthew's wedding waistcoat, 1844.

2.3 The seven children of John and Mary Ann Ann Matthew, l to r, Herbert, George, Kate, Frances, Henry, Arthur and Charles, c 1863.

1851 census, their home was recorded as being above the shop at 25 Trinity Street, the premises the firm initially rented. It was shared with their five children at the time, three living-in servants and a grocer's assistant. John and Mary Ann were to live above their shop for around thirty years. They had eleven children in all but four boys died in infancy, two called Frederick and two called Sidney, all buried at Mill Road Cemetery in their grandparents' grave. All but one of John and Mary Ann's other seven children, five boys and two girls, lived to a reasonable age for the time.

When David returned to London in 1849 it was a natural step for John to take over his partnership with John Gent. Mr Gent died in 1868, leaving John as head of the business. A lease describes him as Grocer, Italian warehouseman and dealer in provisions, china and glass. (Italian warehouseman was the term then used for someone running a delicatessen.)

An active citizen

John played his part in the community as well as developing the family business. He attended All Saints Church, initially next to his shop. The church was pulled down in 1865 and John in time became churchwarden of the new All Saints Church on Jesus Lane. He was a trustee of Forester's Charity and represented Holy Sepulchre Church, the Round Church on Bridge Street, on the Board of the Improvement Commissioners. The Commissioners were a group formed by an Act of Parliament in 1788, with powers to pave, clean and light the streets, which were then often dirty and unpaved. The Improvement Commissioners were in operation for 100 years and only surrendered their powers to the council in 1889. John was also a Trustee of the Cambridge Savings Bank: clearly he was a respected citizen, playing a responsible part in the life of the town.

Creation of Matthew & Son

Two of John's sons, Henry and Charles, had become grocer's assistants, allowing their father to plan the succession. In 1874, when John was 63 and Henry, his eldest son, was 29 they entered into a Deed of Partnership as co-partners in the firm of Matthew & Son, to last for ten years. The Deed of Partnership enshrines the ethical principles of the agreement: 'Each of the said partners will be just and faithful to the other in all accounts.' Henry had become a Royal Navy midshipman at 15, but did not stay in the Navy. In his early twenties he left the sea and began work with his father in Trinity Street, living with his family above the shop until his marriage.

Henry married Margaret Gosling, also in 1874, sister to the Cambridge architect Ernest Gosling, and she and Henry lived at 7 St George's Terrace in Chesterton, built in the mid 1800s. Chesterton, an ancient parish north-east of Cambridge town centre, grew in size in the second half of the nineteenth century, with a series of terraces of solid middle-class houses being built along the north side of Chesterton Road. Henry and Margaret had two children, Harold, born in 1875 and Eva in 1877. His life appeared very settled and the succession seemed assured.

More than a grocer

Henry Matthew became more than a grocer. He was also a successful businessman in other fields, active in good works, a local politician, a writer and debater and a performer of amateur dramatics. His business

2.4 Henry Matthew, c 1875.

interests included the new but short-lived Tramways Company of which he became a Director. It was Henry who proposed the toast to the new company at a dinner held at The Lion Hotel to celebrate the passing of the Cambridge Street Tramways Act on August 7th 1879. He had property interests and owned for a time the Lensfield Estate at the corner of Hills Road and Lensfield Road, a large property with a big house, an orchard, stables and extensive grounds. This was to become the site for the Catholic Church, Our Lady and the English Martyrs, still a landmark in Cambridge with its soaring spire.

Like many other Cambridge businessmen, Henry took an active part in the community. The new YMCA was one of his charitable interests and he became interested in politics, was a founder of the Junior Conservative Club and its first President, and developed a reputation as a public speaker. He became a town councillor, elected as a Conservative to represent Market Ward in 1878, and was also an occasional writer. He published a pamphlet *Shops or Stores?* the following year, 'Exchanging,' as he said, 'for a brief period an apron for a pen,' in which he challenged the role of large co-operative societies such as the Army and Navy Stores. He later presented evidence on the topic to a Select Committee of the House of Commons. The pamphlet sold for 6d and went into a second edition.

As an amateur actor, his performances included taking part in dramatic presentations of The Pickwick Papers, playing the self-important barrister Serjeant Buzfuz. Josiah Chater's diaries, published as *Victorian Cambridge*, provide a vivid insight into life for young businessmen in Cambridge at the time and give a fair idea of Henry's life too. Josiah, originally an apprentice with Eaden Lilley – another well-known Cambridge firm – and later one of the first chartered accountants in Cambridge, was a close friend of both Henry and his younger brother George. Henry was clearly a rising townsman as well as working with his father, learning the trade in preparation for taking over.

A partnership cut short

But on Friday September 12th 1879, at the age of only 34, Henry died of apoplexy. He had gone to Matlock, a popular spa town in Derbyshire, 'taking a respite from his manifold engagements and the cares of the important concerns which he had on hand,' as reported in the *Cambridge Chronicle*. The exact cause of his death is unclear: apoplexy, a term used for a stroke, could also mean any sudden death. Henry had been active till the last, even taking part in an entertainment got up that evening for charitable purposes.

His funeral at Mill Road Cemetery was attended by a large number of people, including employees of the firm, political colleagues, family and friends. His obituary in the *Cambridge Chronicle* records the loss of

SECOND EDITION.

SHOPS OR STORES ?

AN ANSWER TO MR. LAWSON'S PAPER

ENTITLED

"Co-Operative Stores; a Reply to Shopkeepers,"

IN THE FEBRUARY NUMBER OF THE

"Nineteenth Century."

BY

HENRY J. MATTHEW.

>—•◆•—<

"Do I sleep? Do I dream?
Do I wonder and doubt?
Are things what they seem,
Or is visions about?
Is our *Co-Operation* a failure,
Or is the *Retailer* played out?"

PRICE SIXPENCE.

CAMBRIDGE:
W. P. SPALDING, 43, SIDNEY STREET.
1879.

*2.5 A pamphlet written by Henry Matthew –
a lively contribution to a debate on retailing politics, 1879.*

'one of our rising and most prominent townsmen, the borough sustaining a severe public loss, while many persons had been bereft of a constant and honourable personal friend.'

His will, naming Josiah Chater as one of his executors, shows he died a very rich man: his total estate was worth nearly £15,000, a large sum at the time. Among his legacies were gifts to Josiah, Deacons Baptist Church, the Victoria Asylum and the Female Refuge.

So the succession was not as intended and the impact on Matthew & Son could have been considerable. His widow Margaret took over as co-partner with her father-in-law for the remaining five years of the partnership, an arrangement made in Henry's will, but there is no record that she took an active part in the business.

Another 'Matthew & Son'

Henry's younger brother Arthur, who had been sent to a business at Great Yarmouth to learn the stationery and bookselling trade, returned to Cambridge to work with his father. Two of John's other three sons, Herbert and Charles, did not stay in Cambridge. Herbert emigrated to Canada and Charles moved to Brighton and little is known about them. Five years later, a new Deed of Partnership was drawn up between Arthur and John by the solicitors Ginn & Matthew. (The youngest Matthew son, George, had in the meantime trained as a solicitor and joined Ginn's.) Despite the loss of Henry, Arthur was a good choice, the firm remained stable and it was still Matthew & Son.

John and Arthur

Arthur was to show himself a resourceful and imaginative businessman, and the handover between the generations did take place, helped by John continuing to work with his son. Though John had heart trouble for thirteen years and was less active from his early 60s, he remained partly involved in the firm until he died at the age of 77 on October 1st 1889. By then he was no longer living above the shop but had moved to a substantial house at 7 Park Terrace, built in the 1830s by Jesus College, facing south over Parker's Piece. John Matthew had prospered, not only in the Trinity Street firm but through other business interests, for example property. When he died, Arthur was left the grocery business and John's wife Mary

Ann was the main beneficiary during her lifetime of the rest of his considerable estate. On her death – which was to be five years later in 1894 – the estate was to be divided into six equal shares, one each for his five surviving children and one invested for his daughter-in-law, until she married again.

John Matthew's employees all joined his funeral procession. He too was appreciated in his community, for John was widely known, the *Cambridge Chronicle* reports, as:

> An old and valued townsman, a man of good business qualities. He combined these with those characteristics of amiability and benevolence which could not fail to make him beloved by all with whom he was acquainted.

His family also showed their affection and appreciation of John and Mary Ann by endowing a memorial window in the nave of All Saints church in 1905, still to be seen today. Family gravestones in Mill Road cemetery too were liberally funded, with Rattee & Kett being paid £74.16.0 for best Sicilian marble by the family.

While John took on both civic and charitable roles, he is remembered more for his business achievements. Matthew & Gent had been a fledgling business on John's arrival in Cambridge. His importance for Matthew & Son was that by the time he died over fifty years later, it had become firmly established as a family firm. John Matthew weathered the problems of succession, ensured a stable transition to the next stage of the firm's history and passed Matthew & Son on to his son as a thriving business in substantial premises, allowing Arthur to make a sound start to his time in charge.

*2.6 Inscription on a window in the north aisle
of All Saints Church, Jesus Lane, 1905.*

3: LIVING OVER THE SHOP

For two generations of the Matthew family, living over the shop was a way of life, lasting nearly seventy years. Walk along the shopping streets in the middle of Cambridge today, and look up: there are occasional student rooms but it is rare to see that anyone but students now lives above a shop. There are offices, additional sales floors or rooms used by solicitors or recruitment agencies, but no homes, and Cambridge shops are now mostly branches of national chains, not family firms.

Common practice

In nineteenth century Cambridge, the Matthews were not the only family to have their home above their business. It was common for shop owners to do so, bringing up large families and often sharing accommodation with resident domestic staff and apprentices. Some firms used the space for employees to live, with servants to look after them. Eaden Lilley, for example, had rooms for young apprentices, setting down strict rules and employing a lodging keeper to provide the young men with meals, though conditions were not always very good. Josiah Chater, who first arrived in Cambridge at the age of 15, describes his difficult experiences in his diaries with feeling.

Mr and Mrs John Barrrett, whose daughter Agnes was to marry Josiah, lived above their woollen drapery shop on Market Street, sited conveniently for the young couple just next to Mr Lilley's. Robert Sayle, the founder of what was to become John Lewis, did the same when he started off in 1840, and the firm used rooms for their staff above their extensive premises on St Andrew's Street well into the time of the Second World War. Entrepreneurs setting up in business would take opportunities to save money and time by living on the job. It brought benefits of convenience, cheapness, security and for some employers, a means to recruit young staff from outside Cambridge – and guide their lifestyle.

Risks and benefits

But living above the shop was not without its risks, of which fire was one. In 1895, Arthur Matthew was living above the grocery shop on Trinity Street with five bachelor members of his staff and a resident cook-housekeeper. In the early hours of March 9th he was woken by a commotion in the street, described by the *Cambridge Daily News*:

> Residents in Trinity Street were awakened out of their sleep by shrill screams as of females in distress, the blowing of policemen's whistles and hoarse cries of 'Fire'.

The tobacconist's shop and lodging house at number 18, immediately next door, was ablaze. Arthur was one of the first on the scene around 3.0 a.m., one of a number of men who 'rendered valuable assistance', as another detailed account in the *Cambridge Chronicle* reported. There was no 999 to ring. Night porters from Trinity poured water on the blaze and the Volunteer Fire Brigade's Captain, telephoned by the Police Station, came quickly. Its members, summoned by call boys, and a fire escape arrived eventually, but two people died despite everyone's efforts. The widowed lodging-house keeper and her servant, just 16 years old, who had arrived only the previous week, were asleep in bedrooms on the second floor. They were unable to get out and the fire escapes, ladders mounted on wheels, were not long enough to reach them in time.

Arthur was to become more involved later the same day when the inquest was opened and he was appointed foreman of the jury, taking an active role in questioning those involved. The house was completely gutted and the shop was not insured. Matthew's was very lucky that the fire did not spread to their shop next door and to the living accommodation above. Later the same year Arthur was elected as a councillor and in due course became Chairman of the Volunteer Fire Brigade. Perhaps his experience in 1895 led him to offer to take on this role. Later Matthew's installed a hydrant in their yard and held regular fire drills.

While fires were far from uncommon, floods were also a risk. It would have been reassuring to have family or staff living above shop premises, on the spot to deal with such problems. In the summer of 1897 for example, a huge storm brought 3 in. of rain in six hours

*3.1 'Scene of the conflagration' at 18 Trinity Street,
next to Matthew & Son, Cambridge Daily News, March 9th 1895.*

with 'hailstones as big as plums and hen's eggs' and the river rose by 8 ft. Shops were badly affected, particularly the drapers Eaden Lilley, Stockbridge and Robert Sayle, all of which lost stock and had hurried sales of damaged goods, though Matthew & Son was not affected.

But there were serious health risks for all town centre residents. Living conditions in the centre of English towns in the mid to late

3.2 Matthew & Son's shop and living accommodation, 20 – 21 Trinity Street, taken by Charles Porter c 1885. Arthur Matthew is behind the second window from the left.

nineteenth century were generally poor, at times appalling, and in 1848 and 1849 an epidemic of the malignant Asiatic cholera, as it was known at the time, reached Cambridge and several local people died. A preacher at St Michael's Church on Trinity Street attributed the outbreak to God's displeasure with the nation. Dire sanitation systems and the drinking of sewage-polluted water were, however, more accurately to be blamed. In 1848 an Inspector of the Central Board of Health had published a very critical report, but at a public meeting a resolution was passed that no improvement was wanted. Cambridge did not take kindly to change.

The dirty streets were largely unpaved and while there was no motorised traffic until the early twentieth century, the centre of Cambridge was not a peaceful place to live. Cobbled streets were busy with rattling handcarts, clattering horse drawn vehicles and bicycles with bells. Many clocks chimed the hour and Great St Mary's tolled an evening curfew for students.

Mid nineteenth century Cambridge, despite its disadvantages, however, was a lively and friendly place. Living centrally brought many social advantages to shop owners, their families and their staff, giving them easy access to entertainments, lectures, churches, parties, friends and family. Many residents enjoyed a busy social life, despite long working hours, and there were often close friendships and personal links between business people living in the centre. There were memorable events too, such as the royal visit made by the young Queen Victoria to Trinity College in 1843, when triumphal arches were erected across the street. David Matthew and his family, living opposite, were well placed for viewing her arrival.

The Matthew family

By the time of the census in 1841, David Matthew, his wife Elizabeth, three small children, a 17 year old apprentice and three female servants were all living above the premises, then at number 25 Trinity Street. By the time of the next census, in 1851, David had left for London and John and Mary Ann, their family, servants and an assistant were resident.

The space above the shop they moved to in 1858 was larger. The premises, formerly known as Baxter's, initially included two buildings, numbers 20 and 21 Trinity Street, spreading across a frontage measuring 32 ft. and extending back a long way towards Sidney Street. Two staircases are shown on a plan of 1875, with the living accommodation on both the first and second floors included in the lease agreed that year. The front first floor rooms had elegant proportions, with plaster cornices and long sash windows with both curtains and fringed blinds.

John's son Arthur spent his childhood and much of his adult life above the shop. He stayed on when his parents moved, living there with staff and servants for another 25 years until he was 48. But unlike his father, Arthur had a retreat, his leisure garden on Mount Pleasant.

End of an era

By 1898 Arthur had moved to his house built on the leisure garden and at the turn of the century Matthew's premises were renovated. Trade was temporarily carried on only at The Café at 14 Trinity Street and no-one was able to live above the shop during that period. In time the rooms above the main shop came to be used as offices, with utilitarian partitions dividing up the elegant first floor rooms. From then on, living over the shop, with its advantages and its risks, was no longer part of the story of Matthew & Son.

3.3 The grocery and wine shop undergoing major renovation, 1902.

*3.4   Some trade continued at 14 Trinity Street
while building work was carried out, 1902.*

4: ARTHUR MATTHEW OF THE GARDEN HOUSE

Arthur, John's fourth son, born above the shop in 1850, became an important contributor to the development of Matthew & Son but he was also a sportsman, a cyclist, horticulturist, politician and a family man.

Sportsman and gardener

Arthur's photo (see next page) shows him as fit and upright, with an air of confidence. He skated in cold winters when Grantchester Meadows were frozen over, lit by electricity at night. Lamp-posts can still be seen in the middle of fields by the river where the old skating ground used to be. Arthur once skated to Ely when the Cam froze over, returning by train. At bridges and locks and at places where the passage of ferries had kept the water open they had to walk round on land. He played golf and bowls and swam in the river at Newnham in the summer. He was active in the Cambridge Bicycle Club, owning a Sunbeam bicycle, an expensive quality machine first manufactured in 1889, aimed at the top of the market. The Club held races on the Bicycle Path, situated between Madingley Road and what became Adams Road. Its members included other well-known Cambridge men, from both the University and the town, one being Alderman John Death, four times Mayor of Cambridge, while its President at one time was a Fellow of Trinity, Dr J.H. Moxon.

For 17 years Arthur was not only a member but also Honorary Secretary of the Cambridge Horticultural Society, and one of the organisers of the annual show held in the Fellows' Garden of Trinity College or St John's. His interest in gardening might seem surprising for a man born above the shop, and who continued to live there until his late 40s, but Arthur rented a leisure garden. These were designed to give town centre residents a chance to create a quiet garden away from busy streets and to grow fruit and vegetables.

4.1 Arthur Matthew aged about 45, mid 1890s.

*4.2 Members of the Cambridge Bicycle Club at a garden party
at The Garden House. Arthur is seated, second from right, 1880.*

*4.3 Committee of the Cambridge Horticultural Society,
with Arthur, Hon. Sec., seated left, 1896.*

Arthur was one of thirteen tenants of St John's College who
each leased a quarter acre leisure plot for the sum of £7 per annum
as part of Madingley Road Pleasure Gardens. These gardens were
one of seven in Cambridge, sometimes called Leisure Gardens and
sometimes Pleasure Gardens. This one was laid out on land between
Mount Pleasant, where Arthur's plot was situated, and the north
side of Madingley Road. His neighbours were at first mostly other
prosperous businessmen and some senior college servants. Each

plot was individually designed and included a summerhouse, one still existing in the garden of a house off Madingley Road, and each garden had water laid on. Arthur grew vegetables, selling them in the shop, had a bowls lawn and used his garden for entertaining. He held a garden party for members of the Bicycle Club in 1880 and his son Bernard remembers being told that his father used to invite his bachelor friends for bowls and supper in the summerhouse on summer evenings, followed by the singing of glees.

Arthur as businessman

Arthur fitted a lot into his days. As well as having an active social and sporting life, he played an important role over many years in the family business. For part of his education he had been a boarder at Bishop's Stortford College and after this was apprenticed by his father to a firm in Great Yarmouth to learn the stationery and bookselling trade, perhaps with an eye to expanding that side of the business in Cambridge. In 1879, at the age of 29, his life changed dramatically when his oldest brother Henry died suddenly and Arthur took his place.

Arthur worked in the business from then on, agreeing a formal partnership with John in 1884, with John continuing to be involved until shortly before he died five years later. Arthur was left the business in John's will and in 1895 he took a significant step. He established the business as a Limited Company, becoming Governing Director with very wide powers under the company Memorandum and Articles of Association, by which he could control the holding of ordinary shares and the appointment of Directors. The other founding shareholders were the four women members of the family – his two unmarried sisters, his widowed sister-in-law and her daughter, an arrangement most likely planned to ensure they had some income – and two businessmen, one of whose businesses had been absorbed into Matthew's. All six and Arthur initially held just one share each. The document allowed the firm to carry on the business of a general store in all its branches, listing the varied aspects of its trade. The Company's objects were:

> To carry on business as grocers, dealers in china, glass, earthenware and hardware, Italian warehousemen, oil and

colourmen, stationers, grocers, provision merchants, dry-salters, druggists and Birmingham factors, brushmakers, turners and carriers, furniture dealers, and sellers of ales, stouts, wines and spirits.

Some of these terms remain baffling, but clearly not for nothing was the term 'The Stores' emblazoned on Matthew & Son's vans!

Arthur Matthew's period as head of the firm was a time of innovation and expansion: installing a telephone; expanding the ordering and delivery service; renovating the grocery shop premises; taking on the lease of 14 Trinity Street and opening The Oriental Café; and purchasing other businesses. By the early twentieth century it was reported that 150 members of staff were employed. Renovation and expansion required complex negotiations with the Senior Bursar of Trinity College and their architect, somewhat challenging at times but concluded with dignity and appreciation. Arthur was a good publicist and weekly advertisements prominently displayed on the front page of the *Cambridge Chronicle* proudly announced new items on sale. The firm's catalogue of 1913 listing the huge variety of goods on sale shows Arthur as very customer focussed:

> In case of any incivility or want of attention, Customers are requested to communicate personally with the Company. Or by letter marked Private.

Appreciated by his staff, around 1913 his employees presented Arthur with some magnificent silver, 'as a slight expression of their esteem'. His son Bernard, who had a nice sense of humour himself, included a story about his father and his staff in his memoirs:

> He frequently rode his cycle down to business and back, often before breakfast to open the premises. There was an occasion when in the dark at closing time he was bending down blowing up his cycle tyre. Members of his staff were leaving at the time and one of them caught him a resounding blow on the bottom saying 'Goodnight Johnson'. Dad kept down, blowing up the tyre and just saying a cheerful 'Goodnight' so as not to embarrass the person concerned who he never identified.

Councillor, Alderman and active member of the community

Arthur was a town councillor, first elected in 1895, and a member of the Conservative Club of which he became Vice-President and Trustee. He chaired the Fire Brigade Committee and became an Alderman in 1903, remaining active until ill health led to his resignation in 1910. A man clearly prepared to take on responsibilities in the organisations with which he became involved, he was treasurer of Cambridge Municipal Charities for many years, retaining that role until he died. He was also a Trustee of Dame Forrester's Charity and a member of All Saints Church.

Marriage, home and family

Regarded as a confirmed bachelor, as Bernard recalled being told, at the age of 47 Arthur became engaged to Maude Illsley and they were married in 1898. Arthur was twitted by his younger brother George for cradle-snatching, for Maude was only 19 at the time. By that time 99-year building leases on the Pleasure Gardens plots were being negotiated with St John's by some of the garden tenants. Substantial houses were being built on their sites, some by University dons such as 'Elterholm', built in 1888 by Thomas Thornley, a Fellow of Trinity Hall and 'Fossedene' by Dr Hicks, a Fellow of Trinity, to become Arthur and Maude's immediate neighbour. Many of these houses are still in use, now as student accommodation.

Arthur followed his neighbours' example and built a substantial home. 'The Garden House', Arthur and Maude's house built on Mount Pleasant in 1897, was designed by the Cambridge architect Ernest Gosling, Margaret Matthew's brother. Arthur chose the name in a hurry after being pressed to make a decision by W.P. Spalding. Bernard remembered hearing the story of how its name was chosen:

> My parents had had difficulty in settling on a name so they delayed until my father's friend, the stationer and publisher of 'Spalding's Directory of Cambridge', told him that he was just going to press with a new edition and that he must have the name of the house for inclusion in the directory. So in desperation, but with a logical reason, they chose 'The Garden House'. This was in spite of the fact that a house by the river, 'Garden

4.4 The Garden House, Mount Pleasant, early 1900s

House', already existed, built at the bottom of Little St. Mary's Lane, and later to become The Garden House Hotel. There was occasionally confusion over the delivery of letters but the names of both Cayley and Matthew were well known in the Post Office.

Arthur and Maude soon extended their house to accommodate their family and a living-in staff of four. A distinctive cupola was added, designed to link the original building with its extension. Now called Bene't House, for it became a house of studies for Benedictine monks, it is still a well-maintained, substantial building, retaining many original features. It is both the base of The International Society for Science & Religion and home to mature students of St Edmund's College nearby, which now owns the house.

Arthur was known as 'a most genial host' and his garden parties were much sought after. His sociability as a bachelor continued after his marriage in his new home: dinner parties, garden parties, whist drives and singing round the piano were all features of his life.

Maude never knew when he was going to bring home to lunch a business friend who had called on him without any prior notice, though a phone, Cambridge 97, had been installed as one of the early telephones in the town.

He and Maude had three sons. The first, Gordon, born in 1898 became a professional soldier and ended his career a Brigadier. Bernard was born two years later and, after a gap of six years, David in 1906. David studied law and became a London solicitor and was to become active in advising Bernard on legal aspects of running the business.

Arthur spent a lot of time with his older sons: they went together on holiday to Scotland in 1910; he took them skating on Grantchester Meadows; and taught them to play golf at Royston Golf Club, going there by train. Two or three times a week in the summer they would go swimming before breakfast at Newnham. Arthur would take one boy for a distance on the carrier of his bike, while the other boy walked, then return for him, so leapfrogging along the Backs, as Queen's Road is still known.

The last years

He was not to continue as the active sportsman he had been. By 1910 Arthur had to give up his civic role through illness and his last years were spent quietly at home. He suffered from kidney disease and the last picture of him is a little sad, showing Maude pulling him in a bath chair in his garden, Arthur wearing a hat, warmly wrapped up in a rug and with a nurse in attendance.

Arthur Matthew died in 1917 at the age of 66, 'a highly esteemed townsman', as his obituary writer described him. Bernard recalled him as a sincere, thoughtful, kindly and considerate man:

> Though Dad had a well-defined sense of humour it was not on the surface. He had a strong affection for his wife and family and a sense of duty towards the community. He was not given to arguments and discussions and I cannot remember him ever losing his temper.

His obituary extolled his business abilities 'and the splendid establishment in Trinity Street is a memorial of them.' Though such a prominent Cambridge businessman and civic leader, his gravestone in the Ascension Parish Burial Ground on All Souls Lane, a peaceful graveyard tucked away off Huntingdon Road, just says simply, 'Arthur Matthew, The Garden House.

4.5 Arthur & Maude Matthew and an accompanying nurse,
in the garden near the summerhouse of The Garden House, c 1917.

5.1 A full-page advertisement in the Cambridge Chronicle, promoting seasonal goods and advertising the many different departments, December 13th 1922.

5: MARMALADE AND OTHER HOUSEHOLD

ESSENTIALS

Matthew & Son was always well known for the wide range of goods it sold. The firm provided 'Every requisite for a household', as the author of an article in the Cambridge Chronicle described the shop in 1898. There was even a story, also in the article, though probably apocryphal, about a pulpit. A gentleman had a bet with a friend that he could obtain anything at Matthew's, even a church pulpit. The bet was accepted, and won, for the firm had stored in one of their numerous warehouses a pulpit in an excellent state of preservation. The story does not relate whether it was actually purchased or where it was installed. By 1922 the shop had nine different departments: grocery; provisions; glass and china; art; stationery; fruit, flowers and vegetables; wine, spirits and cigars; brushes; and ironmongery. It was remembered as a 'retailing giant' by Cambridgeshire historian Mike Petty. Matthew's advertisements capitalized on the theme:

> The Stores – where in one large modern building you can obtain all your wants with London store prices and selection.

But it was only when the 1913 catalogue came back into my possession that I really appreciated the extent to which these were fair descriptions. The large, dark-green, hardback catalogue is illustrated with fine drawings of amazing household equipment, colour pictures of different types of flitch of bacon, entertaining advertisements and firm advice to customers on making coffee and tea. Its 102 pages, with its index ranging from Acid drops to Yorkshire relish, are more than a prompt for a shopping list; they illustrate a way of life.

The Cambridgeshire Collection holds a similar Matthew & Son catalogue printed in 1936, donated to the library by Dr Glyn Daniel. But it does not have quite the style and visual impact of my pre-First World War publication with its hundreds of illustrations and advertisements. Together, however, they have provided a rich

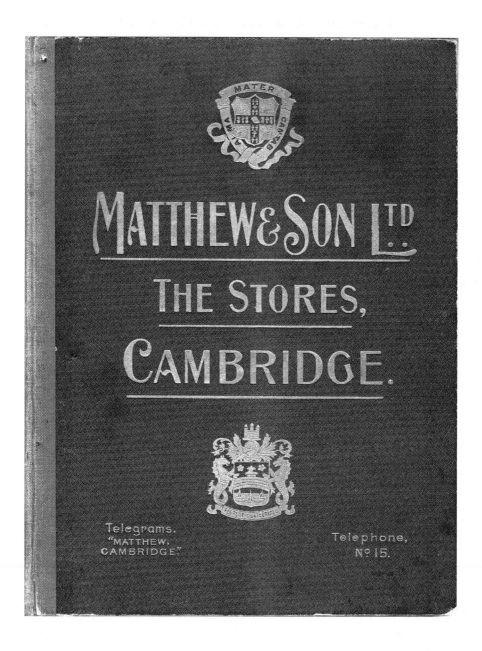

*5.2 The hardback catalogue, with gold embossed lettering,
printed for Matthew & Son's customers, 1913.*

source of information about the huge range of goods Matthew's sold. Included here are just three of them: marmalade; coffee and tea; and brooms and brushes.

Everything but a preserving pan

Making marmalade at home was a well-established British tradition. In other countries, the term marmalade can mean preserves made with fruit other than citrus, but in Britain it was made with tart Seville oranges, high in pectin which aids setting, and made to eat with toast at breakfast time.

MARMALADE
SEASON.

SEVILLE ORANGES,
4s. 6d. PER HUNDRED, 7d. PER DOZEN.

PRESERVING SUGAR,
2s. PER STONE.

MATTHEW & SON, LTD.
TRINITY STREET, CAMBRIDGE.

5.3 The marmalade season had begun. An advertisement in the Independent Press & Chronicle, 1899.

The arrival of Seville oranges in early 1899 in Cambridge was announced by the firm in an advertisement in the local paper. Matthew's expected that their customers, or their cooks, were likely to make marmalade on a grand scale each year, for Seville oranges were sold by the hundred, and preserving sugar, the price of which varied according to market forces, by the stone (14 lb). Many other items were needed for the annual task and Matthew's could provide them all, bar a preserving pan. A large brass or copper preserving pan, recommended by Mrs Beeton as an essential piece of kitchen equipment, would be a once in a lifetime purchase, and one which Matthew & Son did not stock. Perhaps Mackintosh's, the family-run ironmongers on Market Street, had cornered the market.

SOLD BY MATTHEW & SON IN 1913 FOR MAKING, STORING AND EATING MARMALADE,	
• **China, earthenware and glass department**	
1 doz. 1 lb jam jars	1/3d
1 doz. 2 lb jam jars	1/8d
• **Stationery department**	
2 doz. small jam pot covers	1d
2 doz. medium jam pot covers	2d
2 doz. large jam pot covers	3d
• **Grocery department**	
Large wooden spoon	8d
14 lb preserving sugar	2/-
• **Ironmongery department**	
Kitchen scales	17/6d
4 pint saucepan	2/9d
Marmalade machine	16/6d
Toast rack, best electro	6/6d
• **China department**	
White fluted marmalade pot designed to hold & conceal a 1 lb jam jar	2/9d
Marmalade pot, best English china with a gold edge, with a college crest	2/9d
• **Greengrocery department**	
Seville oranges, per hundred	4/6d
Seville oranges, per dozen	7d

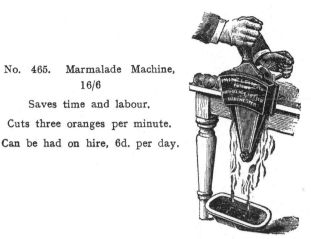

No. 465.   Marmalade Machine,
16/6

Saves time and labour.

Cuts three oranges per minute.

Can be had on hire, 6d. per day.

No. 465.

*5.4 A marmalade machine, for sale or for hire from Matthew's,
from the 1913 catalogue.*

But Matthew's did supply jam jars, jam pot covers, wooden spoons, scales – and a marmalade machine. A marmalade machine was clamped on to a table top, oranges were fed through it and as the handle was turned the oranges were sliced thinly and juice and rind were caught in a bowl set below. It was promoted by Matthew's as a useful gadget which saved time and labour and cut three oranges a minute. As an alternative to buying one, the Hire Department would loan a machine to customers for 6d a day. The service continued, for a customer in Barrington, a village south of Cambridge, remembers the marmalade machine being delivered to her home by the Matthew's delivery van in the 1950s. When her family had finished with it, it was collected and passed on to the next household.

Fifteen varieties

Some customers preferred marmalade ready-made, or just did not have the facilities to make it themselves. M.R. James, an undergraduate at King's in the 1880s and to become a well known author of ghost stories, bought his marmalade ready-made from Matthew's. Customers before the First World War could choose from fifteen varieties, though by 1936 the choice had been reduced to eleven, sold in 1 lb, 2 lb and 7 lb jars.

Keiller's, the Dundee firm where Seville marmalade is thought to have originated, and Cooper's Oxford were among the most expensive, while cheapest in 1913 was Chivers orange marmalade at 4½d a pound. If a customer needed larger quantities, a 7 lb earthenware jar could be provided, but with an extra 3d to be refunded on the jar's return. Chivers had begun to manufacture jam in Histon, near Cambridge in 1873. By 1885, to ensure a permanent, not seasonal, experienced workforce, they diversified into marmalade. Matthew's sold many different Chivers' products and endorsed them in their 1936 catalogue: 'We can thoroughly recommend all Chivers pure food products.' The two families, the Chivers and the Matthews, came to know each other well and met socially.

Two other manufacturers, Ticklers and Cairns, both made somewhat extravagant claims: 'Absolutely pure', and 'Cairns marmalade is the best'. Matthew's offered their own 'home-made' variety, produced in the bakery on Green Street, and Matthew's special Training Marmalade, 'finest quality, prepared with a small proportion of sugar'.

Marmalade was known colloquially as 'squish', a term thought to have derived from nineteenth century public school slang, and Training Marmalade was fondly recalled by Cambridge men, as shown in a letter to the *Sunday Times* in 1950:

> Sir – Mr S.C. Robert, in his review, refers to 'Squish'. This term for marmalade is still used by Cambridge men and their families all over the world. What a poor substitute it is today, with its over-sweetness and lack of the flavour of the orange, especially that of the Seville variety. The glorious flavour of the Training Marmalade made by Matthews those long years ago is but a memory. This was the original 'Squish'. W. Arnold Middlebrook, Hull

The aroma of coffee

A common fond memory of Matthew & Son is their coffee, with Cambridge residents still nostalgically recalling the aroma of coffee wafting out into Trinity Street from the roasting machine in the window. The tale goes that Trinity College indeed once complained about the smell. But the firm made no concessions to its landlord – it was clearly proud of this aspect of its trade, making coffee roasting a feature of the shop and offering to show the process to anyone interested. Their knowledge was enhanced when Fred Cross, a Director of Cross, Sons and Absalom, Tea and Coffee Merchants of Mincing Lane, London, joined the board as a part-time Director in the early twentieth century. His expertise and advice was particularly useful in the period after 1917, when Arthur Matthew had died and before Bernard Matthew took over as Managing Director.

All coffees except proprietary brands were bought in bulk from a wholesaler as green beans, then roasted and ground on the premises daily. The roasting machine had 'all the latest improvements, whereby the pure natural flavour and aroma are retained.' One of Arthur Matthew's four grandsons, Michael Matthew, continues the family tradition. Michael, who has been selling coffee and tea on Cambridge Market for over 20 years, explains the roasting process:

> Green coffee beans are roasted in a drum that rotates around a wire mesh spindle with a gas flame inside. After about fifteen minutes the bean doubles in size, the coffee crackles and the changes in its chemistry produce aromatic oils with the familiar smell and taste of coffee. The coffee then either falls into the cooling tray or is heated further till it spits out its oils to give it a high roast.

Matthew's wanted their customers to enjoy their coffee, advising them that:

> A cup of good Coffee can only be obtained by:-
> 1. Buying good Coffee
> 2. Having it Fresh Roasted
> 3. Having it Fresh Ground

Each purchase was freshly ground for the customer, unless they preferred beans. The choice grew over the years, from seven blends in 1913 to thirteen different kinds of 'Matthew's Famous Coffees', as they were promoted, being offered in 1936. Blending was an art. A carefully kept notebook dating from 1927 shows a hand-written record by each blender detailing exactly what coffee went into each blend. Tom Peers, the coffee and tea blender from the 1920s, was followed by Bernard Matthew from 1943. Most coffees were blends:

Empire Blend, Fine Blend or Costa Rica for example, and Café Blend, used exclusively in Matthew's restaurant, while some blends were developed for individual customers such as the University Arms Hotel and Magdalene Kitchen. As well as Matthew's own blends, proprietary brands were sold, including Maxwell House, tins of Red, White and Blue French coffee, and even Camp Coffee in a bottle, which had a high proportion of chicory.

Coffee came from many different countries, including Cameroon, Madagascar, Belgian Congo and Tanganyika, though during the Second World War not all of them could be obtained. 'Use Grade 2 Belgian Congo when Madagascar all gone', wrote Bernard in 1945. The most expensive of the single coffees was Blue Mountain from Jamaica, retailing at 3/6d a pound in 1936, over twice the price of Pure Kenya at 1/8d.

Canisters, mills, pots and cups and saucers

Matthew's recommended that freshly roasted and ground coffee be kept airtight. Household canisters lettered COFFEE were sold to store 1–2 lb of ground coffee, or beans if customers preferred to grind their own. Two types of hand operated coffee mill were available in 1913, one free-standing and one secured to a table top like a mincer. By 1959, Matthew's was offering a Moulinex coffee mill, 'a small

No. 324. Coffee Mill. 5/-, 6/6   No. 325. Coffee Mill. 4/-, 4/3

5.5 Coffee mills sold by Matthew's, 1913.

electric grinder for home use, giving complete control over coarse or fine grind'. The firm still offered advice:

> We cannot stress too strongly the advantages of buying your coffee frequently from freshly roasted stocks and transferring to an air-tight container as soon as possible.

A variety of coffee pots or jugs and strainers could be obtained in the China Department, the jug method being Bernard's preferred method at home. In the Ironmongery Department there were Circulation Coffee Machines, a type of percolator, for sale, some of them huge, holding up to 12 cups and 3 pints, with names such as the Varsity Cafetière, the Simplex Cafetière and Queen's Improved. Prices ranged from 1/6d for the simplest to 25/- for the largest. Cona coffee machines, still on sale in 1959 in eight different versions, some with a spirit lamp to keep the coffee hot, were recommended. By then

—THE—
SIMPLEX
CAFETIERE.

THE MOST SIMPLE
and economical Coffee
Machine on the Market

No. 317.
Pints ..	1	1½	2	2½	3
No. 317. All Brass, with glass cover	11/6	13/-	14/6	15/6	16/6
No. 317a. Brass, black handle, glass cover	9 6	11/-	12/-	13/-	14/-
Glass cover only ..	7d.	8d.	10d.	1/-	1/3

5.6 The Simplex cafetière, 1913.

they were double the price they had been in 1913. Breakfast cups and saucers, and smaller coffee cups for after-dinner coffee, could be bought in the China Department, in a variety of designs and with the option of a college crest on the cups, a popular addition.

A good cup of tea

Matthew's was equally proud of their teas, offering advice on making this too:

> The greatest care is exercised to select only first-class Teas of early pickings, which are specially suited to the water of this district. The result of many years' experience enables us to give our customers best possible value for money... To obtain a good Cup of Tea care should be taken that the water should be poured on immediately it boils. The reason Tea is often flat and flavourless is that the water is overboiled.

The range of blends of teas grew from seventeen in 1913 to twenty three in 1936. Special China tea was offered in lead-lined Caddies, the most expensive being Lapsang Souchong, sold at 5/- per lb in 1936. China tea was thought to be good for you: 'Recommended by the first Medical Authorities to be used by all with dyspeptic tendency'. Blends, revised at intervals, were carefully recorded in the same notebook as coffee: Café Blend, for example, was made up of named proportions of Darjeeling, Ceylon and Assam teas. Tom Peers, the coffee blender, was also the tea blender, succeeded in 1943 by Bernard Matthew and from 1946 by Herbert Sadler. Mr Sadler, who was to stay working with the firm for 41 years, was also in charge of the coffee roasting machine in the window.

Matthew's also sold all that was needed to keep, make and drink tea. A tea canister; tea pots, ranging from the Plain Brown Rockingham to more elaborate ones with matching hot water jugs; a tea strainer; and cups and saucers were all available. A twelve-person tea service could be bought, or hired, containing forty pieces: cups and saucers, plates, a slop basin, a cream jug and cake plates. 'At Home' afternoons were a common way of entertaining in Edwardian Cambridge and three-tier wicker cake stands and paper doilies were offered. In the summer, tea baskets were sold for picnics and punting trips on the River Cam.

COLLEGE CHINA.

Best English China, Gold Edge, Arms in Proper Colors.

			s.	d.				s.	d.
Breakfast Cups and Saucers	..	per dozen	20	0	Covered Muffin Dish ..	..	..	4	0
Tea Cups and Saucers	..	,,	12	0	Hot Water Jug, metal swing lid	..		3	6
Coffee Cups and Saucers	..	,,	12	0	Teapot Stand, square or round	..		1	0
Plates, 7 in. (measure 7½ in.)		,,	12	0	Marmalade Jar and Cover	..		2	9
Tea Plates, 5 in. (measure 6 in.)		,,	9	0	Afternoon Tea Service, 4 cups and saucers,				
Egg Cups	..	,,	5	0	teapot, sugar and cream	..	..	9	0
Slop Basin ..	..	each	1	10	Afternoon Tea Service, 6 cups, &c., &c.			11	0
Sugar Basin ..	..	,,	1	8	Butter or Jam Dish, 5 inch	..	..	1	0
Cream Jug ..	..	,,	1	8	Match Vase, light blue	..		1	3
Afternoon Sugar	..	,,	0	8	,, ,, brown	..		1	0
Afternoon Cream	..	,,	0	10	Ash Tray, 3 inch	..	..	0	6½
Cake Plate ..	..	,,	1	8	,, 4 inch	..	..	0	10
Milk Jug ..	..	,,	2	0	Candlesticks, terra cotta, 4½ inch	..		1	3
Teapots	..	2 pints ,,	4	3	,, ,, ,, 6 inch	..		1	9
,,	..	1½ ,, ,,	3	9	Spills, terra cotta, 4½ inch	..	..	1	0
,,	..	1 ,, ,,	3	0	Candle Screens	..	per pair	2	6

5.7 Nine different tea services were on sale, the prices ranging from 11/- to 24/-, 1913.

5.8 *Matthew & Son always had a large China Department, known for its high quality goods, date unknown.*

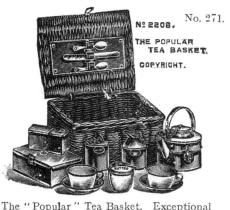

No. 271.

Nº 2208.

THE POPULAR
TEA BASKET.

COPYRIGHT.

The " Popular " Tea Basket. Exceptional
value. Screws to kettle to carry water when
travelling. Good and substantial fittings.
No. 2208. For 2 persons, 12½ × 9½ × 6 14/6
    ,,   ,, 3 ,,   ..   15/6
    ,,   ,, 4 ,,   ..   22/–

*5.9   The Popular tea basket included a kettle, allowing a fresh
cup of tea to be brewed when picnicking, 1913.*

Brushes and brooms

To complete this account of just a few of Matthew's many goods, the
brush department. It was common for Victorian households to possess
a very large number, each designed for a different task involved in
keeping a home, heated by open fires, clean and shining. Matthew
& Son supplied all that housemaids in big houses and bedders in
colleges could possibly need. (The term bedder is short for bedmaker,
a housekeeper in a college of the University of Cambridge. One bedder
would look after a number of rooms). The Brush Department included
60 different brushes before the First World War, designed for very
specific tasks, such as:

Black lead brushes
for cleaning the hearth

A brush for sweeping the
chimney

Four different banister brushes

Crumb brushes and trays

Curtain dusting

A Turk's head brush
for cleaning the toilet

Six different types of
carpet sweeper

Three brushes for furniture

Carpet brushes

Ceiling dusting

For personal use Matthew's sold hair brushes, also providing a leather case for gentlemen's hairbrushes, toothbrushes and shaving brushes. A shoe brush box kept all that was needed to clean the family's shoes together; pastry brushes were available for the kitchen and decanter brushes for the butler's pantry; and four different brushes could be supplied for horses in the stable.

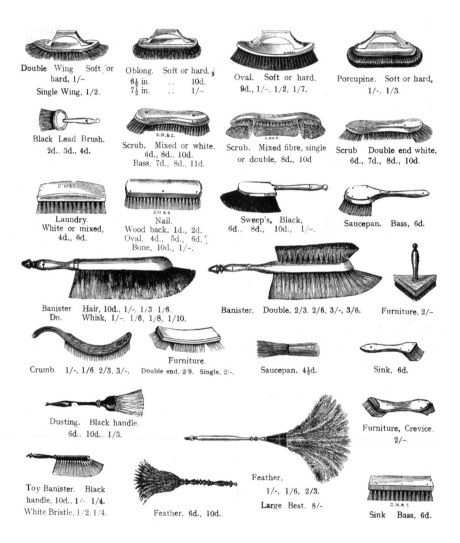

Double Wing Soft or hard, 1/-
Single Wing, 1/2.

Oblong. Soft or hard,
6½ in. .. 10d.
7½ in. .. 1/-

Oval. Soft or hard,
9d., 1/-, 1/2, 1/7.

Porcupine. Soft or hard,
1/-. 1/3.

Black Lead Brush.
2d.. 3d., 4d.

Scrub. Mixed or white,
6d., 8d., 10d.
Bass, 7d., 8d., 11d.

Scrub. Mixed fibre, single
or double, 8d., 10d

Scrub Double end white,
6d., 7d., 8d., 10d.

Laundry.
White or mixed,
4d., 6d.

Nail.
Wood back, 1d., 2d.
Oval, 4d., 5d., 6d.
Bone, 10d., 1/-.

Sweep's, Black,
6d.. 8d., 10d., 1/-.

Saucepan. Bass, 6d.

Banister Hair, 10d., 1/-. 1/3 1/6.
Do. Whisk, 1/-. 1/6, 1/8, 1/10.

Banister. Double, 2/3. 2/6, 3/-, 3/6.

Furniture, 2/-

Crumb. 1/-, 1/6. 2/3, 3/-.

Furniture.
Double end. 2/9. Single, 2/-.

Saucepan. 4½d.

Sink, 6d.

Dusting. Black handle.
6d.. 10d.. 1/3.

Furniture, Crevice.
2/-.

Toy Banister. Black
handle, 10d., 1/-. 1/4.
White Bristle, 1/2, 1/4.

Feather, 6d., 10d.

Feather,
1/-. 1/6, 2/3.
Large Best. 8/-

Sink Bass, 6d.

5.10 Just a few of the 60 brushes on sale in the brush department in 1913.

By 1936, this huge variety of brushes had been reduced by a third, to forty items. The First World War brought many new options for women's employment and large households found it much more difficult to get servants. The invention of the vacuum cleaner in 1901, later to transform how houses were cleaned, had its influence soon after its manufacture. An advertising poster designed in 1906 by John Hassall for the British Vacuum Cleaner Company shows a maid with a hand brush running away from a nozzle thrust through the roof light by a male hand. As vacuum cleaners later came into common use manufacturers and retailers of brushes felt the effect and Matthew's trade in brushes dropped. But the extent to which vacuum cleaners were bought depended on whether houses and colleges had been wired for electricity and even then, how many sockets had been installed. Many households continued to use brooms and brushes for cleaning well into the middle of the 20th century.

In 2009 John Lewis's website revealed they sold forty-one different electric vacuum cleaners with attachments, but only fifteen manual sweepers, brushes, mops and dusters. In marked contrast to today, brushes and brooms were an important item of Matthew's stock, and for their customers, part of a way of life.

6: MATTHEW'S CAFÉ – A PLACE OF QUIET REFINEMENT

The Oriental Café Is Now Open proclaimed a prominent advertisement on the front page of the *Cambridge Chronicle* of October 23rd 1896. Over sixty years after they had first started trading further up Trinity Street, Matthew & Son branched out from their original business and also opened The Oriental Café at 14 Trinity Street. Trinity Street was still a prime site, known at the time as having one of the best positions in town. Number 14 was a late sixteenth century timber-framed and plastered house, previously Foster's Bank and before that The Turk's Head Coffee House. Now Jigsaw, a women's clothes shop, it is still a striking and attractive building.

In 1896 Arthur committed the firm to a 21-year lease of the premises from the Foster brothers (still the firm's bankers), at £300 per annum, one of the conditions of the lease being that Matthew's was not allowed to use any part of the building as a bank. Substantial internal improvements were made to turn it back from a bank to a café, work carried out first in the late 1890s and then early in the twentieth century.

From an oriental atmosphere to Palm Court

'Oriental Cafés' were fashionable in a number of towns at the time, including Nottingham, Dublin and Belfast. Matthew's carefully planned the design of their new venture to reflect its name, though one modern feature of The Café was that the premises were lit throughout by electric light. The décor made prominent use of the star and crescent and a contemporary report in the *Chronicle* describes its ornate design (in ornate language):

6.1 Sketch of 14 Trinity Street, then Foster's Bank, late 19th century.

The Café is handsomely furnished and decorated on arabesque lines. The dado is hand-painted and in the ornamentation of the ceiling Caliph's seals are inserted with excellent effect. The star and the crescent are very much *en evidence* in the decorations. Beautiful pottery adorns the ledges and ferns are suspended in richly gilded flower pots from the ceiling.

Nearly twenty years later, *The Great-North Magazine* featured the business in an illustrated article in 1913, describing the café as:

The finest by far in the Eastern Counties, with all its various apartments, all beautifully furnished, the snow-white table linen, the spruce waiting maids.

By the 1920s the ambience had changed. The Café no longer featured oriental themes but instead included a frieze of college crests, with fresh flowers on each table, while upstairs the decoration of the Oak Room made a feature of the original oak beams. The name had changed by then from Oriental Café to simply The Café or sometimes Matthew's Restaurant and a new lease had included upstairs rooms as well, allowing expansion on to the first floor and the opening of The Oak Room. The Antiquarian Society visited The Café in 1927, reported in the *Cambridge Daily News*:

The fascinating experience of lunching in Cambridge in the atmosphere of our Elizabethan forefathers is made possible by the opening of new rooms at Messrs Matthew's Café. They have turned rooms which were formerly part of a lodging house into a charming medieval retreat. The original beams and window frames remain as well as some beautiful old carvings and the rooms have been furnished in the style of the period, pains having been taken to secure faithful reproductions even down to lamps and pewter pots.

Later, local author Sara Payne recalled its Palm Court atmosphere, with wicker chairs and the rotunda in the ceiling, and other customers remember a piano playing at tea time. Floral china was used to serve tea, and two-tier cake stands, complete with paper doilies, were carried carefully to the table for customers to choose from a selection of

6.2   A change of décor. By the 1920s, the Café displayed college shields.

6.3   The Oak Room on the first floor, opened 1927.

6.4 A plate from the set used in Matthew's Café between the wars.

fancy cakes. The author of a note included on the back of a 1950s menu wrote, 'It is the quiet refinement of the place that makes it so attractive to so many.'

Café customers

When The Café first opened, the menu notes say, it was the only one which catered for the needs of both the University and the town, and 'it still continues its service to the elite.' It was a busy place. Businessmen and women came for lunch; it was a favourite rendezvous for Cambridge ladies for coffee or tea with their friends; and farmers coming into town on business used it as a regular meeting place. Bernard Matthew, Managing Director from the mid 1930s, walked

6.5 The Café, described as 'The farmers' retreat', was where farmers from the Corn Exchange would go for lunch, 1913.

along from his office to The Café twice a day, remembered by Joyce
Bailey, who worked as a cashier there before the Second World War,
'I remember your father came in every morning for coffee, 4d a cup
and also for lunch, 1/9d three courses.' At tea time Bernard had a
cup of tea at his desk.

There were many private functions too. The Café did not serve
evening meals to the public but the premises could be used for private
events. Upstairs rooms, including one seating sixty-five people, could
be booked for private occasions in the daytime or in the evening. The
Cambridge Rotary Club initially met there when it was first founded
in 1922, Bernard Matthew being an early member. Members of the
Cambridge Motorboat Club in 1923 and the National Federation of
Sub-Postmasters in 1924 met in Matthew's Café for their annual dinners.

The Café was used for wedding receptions, children's birthday
parties (Catherine Sharp remembers how she longed to have her
birthday party there for years and years but had to wait until she was
ten), whist drives, family celebrations and parties to mark students'
birthdays. One family, the Simpsons, booked a room to welcome home
their son Harry, who had been a prisoner of war in the Far East, from
the Second World War.

It was not only patronised by local residents but also by members
of the University. Celia Matthew had a joint 21st birthday party with
a friend from Newnham in 1956. The True Blue and Beefsteak Club,
members of which were largely titled undergraduates, booked rooms
at The Café for its elaborate dinners. A True Blue Club menu of 1931
includes oysters and roast partridge salad, with orange ices to clear the
palate between courses. At his first meeting a new member had to drink
a bumper of claret – an extra large glass brimming with wine – straight
off. The Café was the venue when Jack Jones MP and on another
occasion, Jennie Lee, addressed the University Labour Club between
the wars, both lively meetings, arousing great enthusiasm. Earlier on,
before the First World War, there had been weekly fundraising events,
when Arthur Matthew welcomed undergraduates to give concerts on
behalf of Addenbrooke's Hospital, raising nearly £20.

Catering was also undertaken by Café staff in private houses, halls
and outdoors. The Bumps, as the rowing races on the river Cam are
known, provided an opportunity to advertise their services.

6.6 Matthew's catering service and Café advertised in the Race Card for 'The Bumps', June 4th 1919.

After the Second World War, the ESU, the English Speaking Union, took over some of the upstairs rooms and ran a social club called Interclub. Its staff were young women who recall their time there and their lively social life with nostalgia. Members of the Blue Boat, the crew who rowed in the annual boat race against Oxford, became friends of theirs and turned out to be excellent bouncers when uninvited guests arrived at a party at The Café. They remember that the Club rarely bought their ingredients from Matthew's shop, as their prices were too high for the ESU's strict budget, except for frozen peas as an occasional treat, carefully rationed out, which Matthew's supplied.

The menu

The menu at The Café was extolled by the author of the 1913 article in *The Great-North Magazine*: 'The daintily prepared viands would gladden the heart of the most luxurious Epicure.' The Tariff and Specimen Menu included in the firm's catalogue of the same period

THE CAFÉ.

TARIFF.

	s.	d.
Cup of Coffee with Cream	0	2
Large do. do.	0	4
Black Coffee with Lemon	0	2
Tea, freshly made for each Customer in teapot, with Cream	0	3
Tea with Lemon	0	3
Cup of Chocolate	0	3
Do. Cocoa with Cream	0	3
Scone and Butter	0	2
Roll and Butter	0	2
Bread and Butter, White per plate	0	2
Do. Hovis ,,	0	2
Toasted Muffins each	0	3
Do. Tea Cakes ,,	0	3
Toast, Hot Buttered	0	2
Cakes (various) 1d. and	0	2
Jam or Marmalade	0	2
Cream	0	1
Butter	0	1
Biscuits	0	1
Sandwiches—Potted Meat, Fish, &c.	0	2
Omelettes, Savoury or Sweet each	0	8

Specimen Menu.

SOUP.

	s.	d.
Juliene	0	6
Tomato	0	4
Ox Tail	0	6

FISH.

	s.	d.
Filleted Lemon Sole and Sauce	0	10
Salmon Mayonnaise	1	6

HOT.

	s.	d.
Roast Duck and Apple Sauce	1	6
,, Beef and Yorkshire Pudding	1	0
,, Veal and Bacon	1	0
Calves' Liver and Bacon	1	0
Lamb Sweetbreads and Peas	1	0
Steak and Kidney Pie	0	10

COLD.

	s.	d.
Spiced Beef	0	8
Roast Lamb and Mint Sauce	0	10
Ham and Tongue	0	10
Chicken and Ham (Wing 1/6)	1	3
Galantine Veal	0	10

VEGETABLES.

	s.	d.
Salad	0	4
French Beans	0	3
Vegetable Marrow	0	2
New Potatoes	0	2

SWEETS.

	s.	d.
Raspberries and Cream	0	6
Plum Tart and Cream	0	4
Stewed Red Currants & Rasp. & Cream	0	4
,, Apricots and Cream	0	4
,, Black Currants and Cream	0	4
Apricot, Pineapple and Strawberry Ices 4d. and	0	6

CHEESE.

	s.	d.
Gorgonzola, Gruyere, Cheddar	0	2

BISCUITS.

Home-made Chocolates, Cakes, Confectionery, Hovis and Fancy Bread supplied.
A great Speciality for which the Establishment has become famed, is the display in the respective Seasons of Easter and Xmas Novelties in great variety.

6.7 The tariff and specimen menu offered in 1913.

shows some of the refreshments offered. In 1950 The Café served three-course lunches and light meals throughout the day, with a choice of many different teas and coffees, including Café Coffee, Matthew's special blend. Cold drinks, ices and sundaes were all available. Toasted crumpets were a favourite in winter and the menu also included cinnamon toast, anchovy toast, Chelsea buns and a wide range of fancy cakes from the bakery. Customers could request a high tea too, poached eggs on toast or welsh rarebit. Beers and spirits had to be sent out for but The Café was licensed to sell wine.

Bakery and shop

Matthew's own bakery was initially in the interconnected building on Green Street, turning out 500 cakes a day when it first opened. The bakery was promoted vigorously and 'as only the best ingredients are used we guarantee their absolute purity.' The 1936 catalogue listed just a few of their recommended cakes:

Madeira
Ginger
Sultana
Genoa
Square Fruit
Dundee
Cherry
Tutti Fruit
Raisin
Seed

A large variety of small fancies was available, and as in the Café, Chelsea buns and crumpets, often bought by undergraduates to toast in their rooms at teatime. The bakery later moved to 105 Cherry Hinton Road, where a faded sign can still be seen on a wall, advertising the merits of 'pure machine made bread'. Between the wars a special bread, Matthew's Sunshine Bread, was developed and widely advertised:

Eat and Enjoy MATTHEW'S SUNSHINE BREAD
No amount of care in Kneading, Mixing or Baking can equal the advantages gained by using the Ultra Violet Rays apparatus. Equipment of the latest pattern has been installed and is used to flood the dough with Ultra Violet Rays during mixing every particle of the ingredients and activating the yeast cells. The resulting produce is Bread that
IS EASILY DIGESTED
IS UNUSUALLY RICH IN NOURISHMENT
BUILDS UP BODILY STRENGTH

6.8 A wedding cake made in the bakery, c 1910.

Matthew's wedding cakes were celebrated, wrote the author of the 1913 article, and in 1898 Matthew & Son had been awarded a bronze medal at the Confectioners Exhibition. Its reputation continued, for much later on Margaret Graves, who worked for Matthew's as a cashier, had her wedding cake from the shop.

Matthew's Café was also a shop. On the left, as customers came through the glass door from Trinity Street, tall glass jars of sweets were lined up on shelves on the wall behind the sweet counter. On the right, the counter offered a wide range of cakes to choose from and bread was displayed on sloping shelves on the wall behind the assistant. A cash desk, at the foot of the three steps up into the Café where its customers stopped to pay their bill when leaving, served the shop too.

The Matthew children remember their visits to the shop in the late 1940s and 1950s, to collect a whole month's sweet ration, four ounces per child per week. (But there was no feast when they got home to Caxton. The sweets were tipped into their four sweet tins, put firmly on a high shelf in the corner cupboard and could only be reached down and dipped into after tea each day.) There was plenty of choice, within the limits of the ration book, for there was a nationwide interest in sweets and a huge variety were manufactured. Sweets were rationed from 1942. They were taken off ration in 1949, but only for a four month period, demand having outstripped supply, and sweet rationing had to be reinstated, lasting from 1949 until 1953.

Café staff – and a change of menu

The Café closed soon after the firm was taken over in 1962, leading to redundancy or retirement for the staff. By this time the shop had six

6.9 Mrs Graves, a cashier with the firm, had her wedding cake made in the bakery in 1960.

6.10 The Matthew children, regular customers at The Café and its shop, l to r, Celia, Stephen, Judith (as I am known in the family) and Richard, 1947.

members of staff, one full-time and five part-time and the Restaurant had fourteen full-time and eight part-time employees. They included Miss Blackwell as Shop Manageress, Mrs Stuttard as Manageress of the Restaurant and Miss Cissy Barton as Head Waitress.

The building continued to be known for its food, as The Turk's Head, a Berni Inn, was opened on the site. Berni Inns was a chain of steakhouses which expanded quickly in the 1960s, serving a set menu for 2/6d a head and remembered by customers as being distinctly glamorous. But Berni Inn customers, served a menu of prawn cocktail, steak, chips and peas, followed by Black Forest Gateau, had a somewhat different experience from the previous customers of 14 Trinity Street, who for seventy years had enjoyed the quiet refinement of Matthew's Café.

7: DESPATCH AND DELIVERY

When Bernard Matthew was a small boy in the early 1900s, his father Arthur used to take him and his brother to see the firm's horses stabled behind the shop on their way back from church on Sunday mornings. The buildings and yards rented by Matthew & Son covered an acre, stretching from the shop front on Trinity Street right through to Sidney Street. Two stables, with room for eleven horses and an open coach house for delivery vans were located at the Sidney Street end of the premises. 'The horses are well cared for,' reported *The Great-North Magazine* of 1913, 'in fine condition and well groomed.'

Horse-drawn delivery vans were still the normal method of delivery in the early twentieth century. The first motor had appeared in Trinity Street in 1897, a car owned by Charles Rolls, then an 18 year old

7.1 Matthew & Son had stalls for eleven horses in the stables behind the shop, 1913.

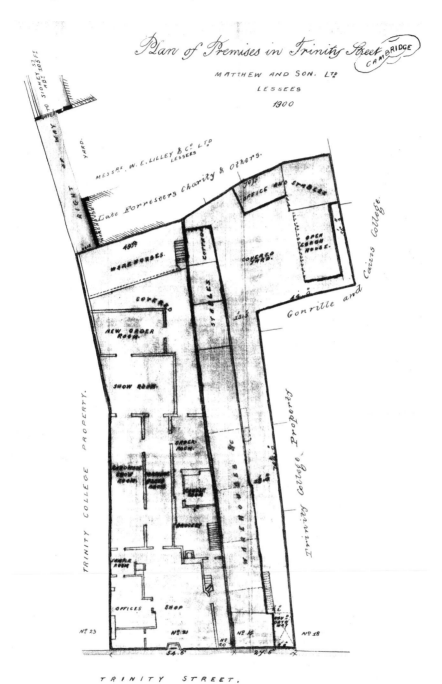

7.2 *A plan of the premises shows two stables and an open coach house for delivery vans, 1900.*

7.3 A horse-drawn delivery van on Trinity Street, with St Johns College in the background, c 1910.

undergraduate at Trinity and later to become co-founder of Rolls-Royce. By 1910 Matthew's had purchased one motor van, a Napier, but still used their eleven horse-drawn vans as well.

Customers' Orders

Orders for delivery could be called for by a member of Matthew's staff. In 1913 orders were taken daily from the colleges and weekly on a regular day of the week in each area of Cambridge, though arrangements could be made for daily calls. Telephone orders could also be given by customers who had phones at home, though it was many years until this was common. Matthew & Son had had a telephone installed in the 1890s, one of the very first in Cambridge. The firm's number was Cambridge 15, with two lines. (George Darwin, second son of Charles Darwin, was number 10 in the Cambridge Directory and his brothers Horace and Frank were 17 and 18.) 'Orders by Telephone have prompt and careful attention' was the firm's commitment. If orders were sent by post and arrived at the shop by first post, they would be delivered by midday, or even earlier if required. The exception was Thursdays, early closing day in Cambridge, a legal requirement from 1904.

7.4 Fifteen men making up orders, packing hampers and boxes and checking lists in the Despatch Department, 1913.

7.5 *Mr Bass, a van driver working for Matthew's in the 1920s, had the use of only one eye but he drove all his life.*

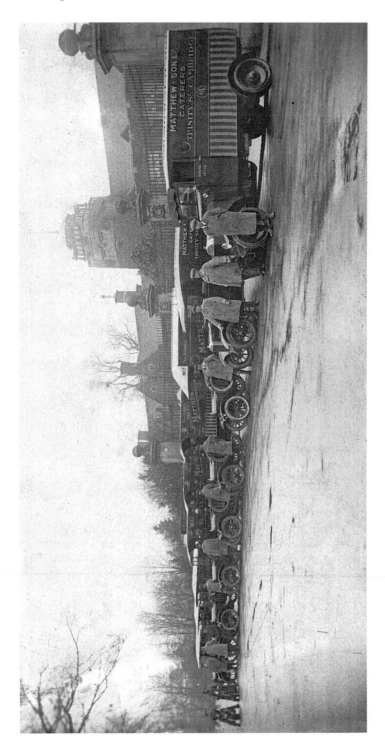

7.6 The fleet of nine vans, outside Westminster College on Madingley Road, 1920s.

7.7 *The motorcyclists (county travellers), l to r, Messrs Charles & Root. The drivers, back row, Edwards, Ashman, Pegg; second row, Gray, Neaves, Sadler, Blows, Reed, Bass, Kitson (van boy); & seated, Jones (mechanic), 1920s.*

COUNTRY DELIVERY AREA by MATTHEW'S MOTOR VANS.

DISTRICT

1	......	......	......	Monday (orders solicited Friday)
2	......	......	......	Tuesday (,, ,, Monday)
3 and 7	......	......	Wednesday ,, ,, ,,

Additional deliveries in No. 7 District each afternoon except Thursday.

4 Thursday (orders solicited Tuesday, except Fulbourn District when orders solicited on Wednesday)

5	......	......	......	Friday (orders solicited Wednesday)
6	......	......	......	Saturday (orders solicited Thursday)

Occasional deliveries are made to Ely and district.

The dotted lines on the map indicate the present boundary of our delivery area, but for intending patrons living outside this, we shall be pleased to arrange for the extension of the Area.

7.8 The delivery area and the regular day for each part of the county, 1936.

Despatch department

Such a level of commitment to prompt deliveries required efficient organisation at the shop. A new despatch department had been created as part of building works undertaken at the end of the 1890s, and a large number of staff worked there. Most deliveries were free, but there were a few exceptions: firewood, dog biscuits, oil, soda, sand, salt and mineral waters, a somewhat surprising set of goods, required payment for delivery. Empty bottles and siphons were collected by the van man, with a request made to customers to put them out as money was lost if they were not returned. An errand boy on a bicycle complemented delivery by van in the town before the First World War.

The 1920s to the 1930s

By the 1920s Matthew's no longer had horses but a fleet of motor vans. An early motor was driven by Mr Bass, who worked for Matthew's in the 1920s. The fleet was photographed assembled outside Westminster College in the mid 1920s, each vehicle with its driver. Two men employed as county travellers rode motorcycles, taking orders from a wide area around Cambridge.

The country delivery area, where vans made regular weekly calls on different days of the week in each district, took in the whole of the county in 1936. The vans went as far as Newmarket, Royston, Huntingdon and Ely and the firm would arrange deliveries even beyond this area for 'intending patrons'. Cambridge and the surrounding area still had daily deliveries, each afternoon except Thursdays.

The 1950s to the 1960s

Regular customers had their own order book. By this post-war period the telephone was more important and the number had changed to Cambridge 4444, with three lines. But customers could also come in and sit comfortably in a wicker chair in the order department, alongside the fruit and vegetable department, while Miss Pamplin, head of department, or one of her staff, wrote down what was needed.

Mrs Joy Amis, who worked in the Shelford Branch for ten years, also went out taking orders. 'I used to go out two mornings in the week collecting the orders from the customers' homes. I enjoyed that very much,' she recalls. A member of staff from Matthew's, Ernie Purkis, took the bus out to Babraham every Thursday morning, remembers a customer, and went round The Close (purpose built accommodation for staff of the Babraham Research Institute), order book in hand. He would sit at the kitchen table to take the order and then catch the bus back into Cambridge. Drivers were remembered for the personal service they gave and the friendly relations that developed. They would

7.9 A later delivery van with Matthew's striped motif and the bye-line: 'Quality – and such good value'.

carry the heavy boxes right into the kitchen, and another Babraham resident recalls that the Matthew's man once found she had left her iron on when she'd gone next door. He was credited with preventing a fire. They gave their over-bouncy dog to him but he too found it over-bouncy and it ended up on a farm.

Vans had distinctive brown stripes by this time, and a local firm, Swainland & Son, was retained as signwriters. Matthew & Son used their delivery vans as a form of advertisement. So much coming and going through the town gave a good opportunity to remind residents of the range of their services and how to contact them.

By the time the business was sold in 1962, there were still sixteen members of staff in the despatch department, half of them part-time, and six drivers and a mechanic were also employed. Despatch and delivery, with its large labour force and fleet of vehicles, was both a significant part of the firm's expenditure and part of their personal service to customers. It remained a feature of Matthew & Son to the end.

8: MAUDE MATTHEW, BUSINESSWOMAN

M aude Illsley, daughter of a Cambridge businessman, married Arthur Matthew in 1898 at the age of just 19. She later emerged from her role as wife, mother and hostess to be a strong influence on Matthew's though, while interested in the firm, she had not been formally involved while Arthur was alive. Her father-in-law, John, had had to take action to ensure family succession earlier in its history. Maude's particular importance in Matthew & Son was again to make sure there was a safe transition to the next generation and to bridge the gap left by the death of her husband until her son Bernard could take over.

Businessman's daughter

It was common in Cambridge for business families to become connected by marriage. Maude did come from a business background – though not from a firm on the same scale or with the stability that Matthew's achieved. Born in 1878, Maude was the second daughter of William and Jane Illsley, one of four children. They lived in Paradise Street and then in Auckland Terrace, off Newmarket Road. Her father was a coal merchant and furniture remover, and was also Parish Clerk of the Parish of St Andrew the Less. A modest business, with an office on Regent Street, it could well have come to an early end without Arthur's help, as Bernard recalls in his memoirs:

> William Illsley used to drive a dogcart – one of that kind which had rather large wheels and the seat was therefore high up. He had the misfortune to be thrown out – I presume the horse shied at something – and broke his thigh. This kept him in bed in hospital and at home for a considerable time. During this time his son Ernest was left in charge of the business, but by the time Grandpa was able to return to it there was no

8.1 Maude Matthew, reputed to have an 18" waist, as a young woman in the late 1890s.

business left but only a stable of racehorses! The upshot was that Ernest was presented with a one way ticket to Buenos Aires. My father helped Grandpa Illsley to get his business on its feet again.

Ernest's sisters were more capable, one becoming a civil servant, another a secretary and Maude proving herself a good businesswoman.

Edwardian hostess

But before her time as head of Matthew's business there were nearly twenty years as wife, mother of three sons and hostess. Maude, an attractive, slim, rather shy-looking young woman became engaged to Arthur Matthew, who was then aged 47. They were married at St Andrew's Church, Chesterton in January 1898. 'An Interesting Cambridge Wedding' was the headline in the *Cambridge Chronicle*, the church being chosen because the wedding breakfast was held at the home of her uncle, John Bester, who lived nearby on Chesterton Road. A local Councillor, his name is still on a plaque commemorating the opening of Victoria Bridge.

Maude and Arthur, after a honeymoon in Brighton, moved into The Garden House, their spacious, newly built home on Mount Pleasant. The couple had four servants, most of whom lived in: a cook, a housemaid, a parlour maid, who was sometimes a daily, and a kitchen maid – and later a nanny. They had a gardener too, who was in time to marry the nanny. Bernard wrote about how his mother coped with the challenges of her new role:

> My mother, being so young when she married, had not much experience of housekeeping and the management of servants, so she was somewhat thrown in at the deep end when she found that she had to entertain relations and business friends of my father's. After the initial stages I understand she was an excellent hostess. She had to manage a sizeable staff and was almost completely dependent on her cook. She had not been adequately taught to cook by her mother, nor was it possible for the mistress of the house to do anything in the kitchen after the menus for the day had been settled after breakfast.

Maude held the keys of a large locked store cupboard in the kitchen from which she would issue the daily requirements, other than perishables. The washing was sent out to Mrs Bailey who lived in Auckland Road and a Matthew's horse-drawn van from Trinity Street would call to collect a large hamper of washing on Monday mornings, returning it on Fridays. There was help from the shop with other household tasks too as a boy from Matthew's came each morning at 8 o'clock to clean the knives and the boots, as Bernard describes:

> There was not any stainless steel in those days so all cutlery was liable to stain and had to be polished regularly in a Kent's knife machine. Six table knives or six dessert knives or one carving knife could be inserted into slots, a handle was turned which was quite hard work, and this turned discs to which Oake's knife polish was applied. Boots were mostly black in those days and the polish was a thick liquid applied to a stiff brush first, then to the leather, then allowed to dry, then brushed vigorously.

Maude took an active part in the social life of her day, holding 'At Homes' and leaving cards with other middle-class Cambridge ladies.

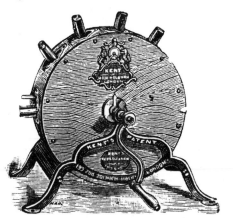

No. 455. Kent's Knife Machine.

2 Knives and Carver	21/–,	32/–
3 do. do.	..	40/–
4 do. do.	–	70/–

8.2 A Kent's knife machine, as sold at Matthew & Son and used at The Garden House, 1913.

8.3 Maude and Bernard having afternoon tea in the large garden at The Garden House, c 1905.

She played bridge and tried her hand at golf. The couple had frequent guests, often staying for a week or two at a time, and would entertain their friends, many of them other business people, at evening social events when Maude would sing traditional songs, such as The Last Rose of Summer. Sunday teatime was always the traditional time for entertaining undergraduates and Maude, being an attractive young woman, was always very popular with them. She and Arthur had three sons. In 1902 the two eldest boys, Gordon and Bernard, were left in the care of the nanny, while Maude and Arthur visited the south of France.

She learnt to drive and became one of the first two woman drivers in Cambridge. The family initially had a carriage but in 1915 they purchased their first car, a Rover 14. The speed limit had been set at 20 mph in 1903, though this was not rigorously enforced. The boys used to have to get out and walk up Madingley Hill, as the car did not

8.4 Arthur & Maude on holiday in Menton, 1902.

have enough power to get the whole family up one of Cambridgeshire's few modest hills.

Maude could drive, and run a business, but did not have the vote. It was not until 1918, when the Representation of the People Act gave women of property over the age of 30 the right to vote, that Maude could vote. By then a widow, she was taking a leading role in Matthew & Son.

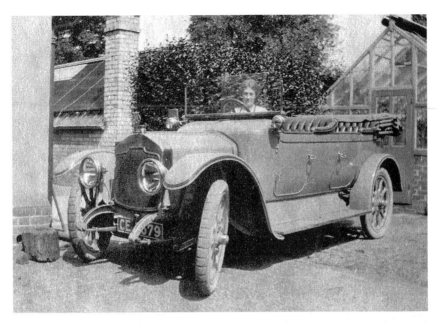

8.5 Maude at the wheel of the family's first car, a Rover 14, 1915.

Widow and businesswoman

When Arthur had died in 1917, Maude, aged 38, had become one of three Trustees for Matthew & Son and Chairman of the Board of Directors under the terms of his will. It was unusual for a woman to chair a Board of Directors, but she was not the first in Cambridge, for Elizabeth Lilley had temporarily been in charge of Eaden Lilley when her husband William Eaden Lilley died in 1837. Arthur had been ill for some years when he died, so there had been time to plan the next stage of the Matthew family succession. Bernard wrote:

> My father had been governing director, with very wide powers under the company Articles of Association by which he could control the holding of ordinary shares and the appointment of Directors. These powers were assumed by the Trustees of his will – Maude Matthew, Fred Cross and Dr. H.B. Roderick. The last named was at the time abroad on war service and withdrew from his trusteeship. My brother Gordon was appointed in his place.

Fred Morgan, previously Office Manager, was promoted to be General Manager with departmental managers under him, and became

8.6 Maude, Chairman of the Board of Directors, in her garden, 1930s.

a Director. Fred Cross, a family friend and London businessman, was to provide crucial support to Maude. At one point he identified weaknesses in the way the routine business of the firm was being managed and firmly intervened to improve staff performance. But Maude, in spite of having no business experience or training, devoted herself thoroughly to its day to day running, managing well with Fred Cross's support. Bernard was to inherit a stable business when he joined the firm in his 20s.

Maude had the ability to think strategically about the future of the firm and did not plunge Bernard into the job straight away. Passing responsibility to this third generation brought a new challenge to the family. Bernard's grandfather and father had each had the chance of many years working alongside their predecessors, easing the time of transition, but this was not possible in Bernard's case, aged only 17 and still at boarding school when his father died after a long illness. With his older brother Gordon already in the army, and the younger, David, only 11, he was the obvious successor. But apart from some months as a trainee, Bernard did not immediately start work. His mother and the firm's Trustees made a wise decision to offer him the chance to take a degree at Clare College, though Maude did require him to live at home with her. This was followed by a time when he learnt his trade in other large grocery businesses and only then did he take on his life-long position at Matthew & Son. This completed his education, grounded him in the retail trade and made succession easier.

He still lived with his mother until he married at the age of 34 and moved to live in Caxton, but Bernard did not take over all the company responsibilities for some years. Maude only handed on the position of chair of the Board of Directors in 1937. She remained a Director until she was 76, in 1954, and was still influential in the decision to sell the business in 1962.

A strong personality

The young woman who had married Arthur in 1898 grew into an imposing older woman with strong views, a somewhat daunting personality when one met her for the first time. She sold The Garden House soon after Bernard's marriage, moving initially to 21 Madingley Road, and then moved between Cambridge and Eastbourne for the rest of her life. She lived for some time at The Garden House Hotel in Cambridge during the war and then in a flat in Eastbourne, but returned to Cambridge when she got frailer and needed more support. Maude never re-married and died at nearly 90, in 1968.

Maude's contribution to Matthew & Son was a significant one. She emerged from a traditional homemaker and hostess role to become a competent businesswoman, bridged a gap on Arthur's death and ensured there was a smooth passing on of responsibility to the third and last generation of the family to run the business.

9: BERNARD MATTHEW – CITY STALWART

While his predecessors had largely learnt their job from older members of the family, Bernard Matthew, as well as taking a degree at Cambridge, gained his initial knowledge of the grocery trade from other firms. In August 1921 he started work, but not in Trinity Street, instead on a management placement at Harrods, the London department store. 'The system is colossal', he wrote, recording his impressions meticulously – and typically – in a small black notebook, 'and it is rather wonderful as very few mistakes seem to be made.' He learnt how invoices were dealt with, how ledgers were kept and the work of the dissecting office, which analysed sales and fed figures to each department daily. A turnover of over £6 million per year! He also worked for a period at Grimbly Hughes, the renowned Oxford grocer, but it was Harrods' systems which impressed him and he observed too how staff were supported and rewarded and the importance of managers' encouragement and praise.

An Edwardian childhood

Bernard's childhood had mirrored that of many of the prosperous customers of Matthew & Son. The middle son of Arthur and Maude, he was born in 1900. His spacious home, The Garden House, with its large garden, was in contrast to his father's childhood above the shop. A nanny was employed for the three boys and Bernard wrote in his memoirs:

> It included a nursery wing, our nurse was in charge and meals were sent up to us in the day nursery. The wing had a bathroom with a hand basin and hot and cold water and there were fireplaces in all the bedrooms but these were not usually lit unless someone was ill in bed.

9.1 *Arthur and Maude's three sons, l to r, Gordon, David and Bernard, 1908.*

9.2 Bernard aged 7, with fellow pupils at Miss Sharpley's school, 1907.

The boys were not always entirely well behaved and, when older, they would climb out on the roof by the cupola. On another occasion, sent to sit in the sitting room in their best white sailor suits to wait quietly till going out, Gordon and Bernard instead decided to investigate the fireplace – and the chimney, ending with both of them smeared with soot. We children loved hearing stories about this unexpected side of our father, who we saw as rather different, as serious, responsible and orderly.

As a small boy he had attended Miss Sharpley's day school in a terrace house at 27 Halifax Road, off Huntingdon Road, but aged 8, Bernard was sent away to board with Gordon at a private prep school, Lindley Lodge. A letter home informed his parents that 'There are about forty-two more hours, two thousand five hundred and twenty more minutes, one million fifty one thousand two hundred more seconds till the end of term.' At the age of 13, he moved to Eastbourne College where he stayed until his father died in 1917.

Cambridge graduate
At the age of 17, working briefly as a trainee in Matthew & Son, Bernard learnt book-keeping and office work as followed in the firm,

9.3 *Bernard was in the Clare College crew rowing at Henley in 1919, seated, far left.*

9.4   Bernard Matthew, the last Managing Director of the firm, 1930s.

but in 1918 he enrolled at Clare College, Cambridge, the first of his family to go to university, and took a degree in economics and chemistry. Unusually, he continued to live at home. The Clare College Boat Club, just starting again after the First World War, quickly became one of his enthusiasms. Bernard rowed in bow position in Clare's first boat and at Henley, and became Club secretary and a coach. When he graduated he kept up his links with Clare and helped to organise a special dinner for the Boat Club centenary in 1931. His college obituary records that he was particularly proud of his role as a link between town and gown, one which would have been advantageous in his dealings with the University.

He developed many other interests as a young man: theatre, golf, skiing, photography and sailing were among them. He and Gordon bought an old sailing barge and sailed it on the East coast and later across the North Sea, learning navigation and how to deal with sudden squalls, though on boats he could become short-tempered if his crew did not jump to orders, as his children discovered.

Life-long Rotarian

Bernard was a very early member of The Cambridge Rotary Club, which had been formed in 1922, initially meeting at Matthew's Café. He was only 23 when he joined, a young age to become a Rotarian, served as Secretary several times and at 34 became its youngest President. Rotary gave him the chance to meet other Cambridge businessmen and later to travel to other parts of Europe. Rotary lunch each Tuesday at the Dorothy Café remained a weekly routine for Bernard until shortly before he died. He was the oldest member at the time and the longest serving member of the club.

Marriage

His personal life changed in 1933 when he met Enid Doughty, a young actress, through friends in the Cambridge business community, Steve and Dora Stephen. Within a year they had married after a long-distance courtship, as Enid by then was touring, playing in musicals such as Noel Coward's Cavalcade. The marriage between the businessman and the actress in 1934 came as something of a surprise to the Cambridge community he was part of – and it was perhaps a surprising marriage,

9.5 'Rotary President Weds – a brilliant wedding' was the Cambridge Evening News' headline. Bernard and Enid's wedding at Christchurch, Mayfair, London, 1934.

but one which worked. They rented The Thatched House at Caxton, 10 miles west of Cambridge, just for a year initially and later bought it from the Cambridge Preservation Society.

Local businessman

After his attachments to Harrods and Grimbly Hughes, in 1923 Bernard began his forty- year career at Matthew's, initially working with the General Manager. It was not until 1937, in his late thirties, that he became Managing Director.

He was remembered warmly by his employees. A member of his staff, Robin Dyson, still recalls him with gratitude fifty years later:

> I was working for Matthew & Son in the late 1950s as a motor fitter, when I was arrested for driving without a licence and for taking a motorbike without permission. My manager told me to go and see the Managing Director. Bernard listened calmly, told me to get a solicitor and to argue the second charge – for I had had permission from my friend to borrow his motorbike to go and see a young lady – but to plead guilty to the first charge. Bernard offered to come and vouch for me in court and he did. I could have ended up in prison without such good advice and support.

Becoming expert in the many different products the firm sold, including wine, coffee, tea, cheese and bread, he took on a national role in the grocery trade too, making sure he kept up to date with his field. He was both a member of and attended training courses run by the Institute of Certificated Grocers, and became President of its Council between 1947 and 1951. Bernard continued the entrepreneurial approach which was always an important element of the company and made significant contributions to the expansion of Matthew & Son, including the opening of four new branches and the move of the bakery to Cherry Hinton.

Active in his community

Bernard, like his father and his grandfather, took on responsibilities in the community, both in Cambridge and in Caxton. The *Cambridge News'* report of his death carried the headline, 'City Stalwart'. As well

9.6 The Thatched House in Caxton – home to Bernard and Enid for over 30 years, taken in the 1930s.

9.7 Bakery staff, Bernard seated, second left. Mr Tipples, Bakery Manager is standing, far right, 1937.

9.8 *Fellow Rotarians mark Bernard Matthew's 58 years as a member, 1981.*

as having a prominent role in Rotary, he was appointed Justice of the Peace in 1941, serving as a magistrate for 30 years and twice being Chairman of the Cambridge Bench. While on a student placement in the Probation Service in 1964, I had the oppportunity one day to see him dealing with the routine of the Magistrates Court in the Guildhall – and to learn that he was not always quite as organised as his image. There was a delay in the start of proceedings, the Clerk disappeared to ring up Trinity Street and a slightly embarrassed Mr Matthew appeared ten minutes later. As formal as ever in his three-piece business suit, perhaps a little pink from a rather quick walk over from his office, he had just forgotten it was his day in court. As usual he chaired proceedings with formality and fairness.

He was also a Freemason and a Trustee of Hobson's Conduit, the stream which brings water into the City from springs at the foot of the Gog Magog Hills. He became a Trustee of the Trustee Savings Bank, was involved with the Discharged Prisoners Aid Society and was founder-Chairman of the Cambridge Theatre Club. In Caxton he was Churchwarden and Chairman of the Parish Council.

Retirement

With the closure of Matthew & Son, Bernard had the chance for a different life. He started his own small coffee business in Reading and then full retirement later in the 1960s brought the opportunity to travel widely. He remained much attached to Clare College, especially enjoying following the rowing club and in 1981, in his 80s, ringing up to enquire why he had not been invited to the 150th Boat Club celebration dinner, reminding them that he had organised the hundredth. He got his invitation and greatly enjoyed the event. He and Enid moved from Caxton into Cambridge where he continued to help Enid with her drama interests, develop his photographic skills, enjoy good food and wine with friends and family – and to make marmalade each New Year when the Seville oranges arrived. He died at 88 after a short period of illness.

A conscientious, dependable man

He may have taken over from a sense of duty when his father died, but Bernard Matthew never indicated any regret at not having followed an alternative career. He was a calm, conscientious, dependable man with considerable business acumen who led the firm for nearly 30 years. The third and last generation of the family to work in the firm, he saw through further expansion, kept the business running through difficult war-time years and managed the end of the family firm with dignity and competence.

10: WINES, SPIRITS AND TOBACCO

Matthew & Son were as confident about promoting their state-of-the-art premises as they were about advertising the quality and range of their goods:

'The Stores, where in one modern building you can obtain all your wants.'

'The Café premises are commodious and well adapted for their purpose.'

'Matthew & Son have erected an entirely new and much more commodious Despatch Department.'

'The most up to date cellars in Cambridge where wines and spirits are bottled under the most ideal conditions.'

10.1 The interior of the wine shop at 19 Trinity Street, 1925.

The wine shop at 19 Trinity Street (now Heffers Sound), was only small, about 300 square feet, but beneath the wine shop and the extensive ground floor premises of Matthew & Son's grocery shop was a vast cellar with a floor space of 5,000 square feet. Plans for the cellar space to be extended were included as part of alterations to the china department in 1927, when even more space was badly needed and Bernard Matthew wrote to the Senior Bursar of Trinity about their plans, stressing that the firm's need of additional cellars had become a 'matter of urgency'. Customers were invited to tour these cellars, with Matthew & Son assuring them that a visit to see where wines and spirits were bottled would be of intense interest. Their cellars were kept at the best temperature for storing wine, 55°F, still recommended today as the ideal for keeping red wine.

Bottling and bottles

'We hold in stock 2,000 dozens of wines and spirits matured ready for sale as well as large quantities of different vintage wines maturing in bottle here, or in bonded warehouses,' noted the firm in their 1936 price list. (A bonded warehouse was where goods on which the duties were unpaid were stored under bond.) *The Great-North Magazine*

10.2 Racks of wine stored in the cellars below the shop, 1936.

commented in 1913, 'The wine cellar would captivate a Bacchus'. The cellars were used to store wine purchased already bottled, but also in large quantities for bottling on the premises. The firm bought wine from its suppliers in bulk in large barrels, some shipped from even as far away as Australia, including a number of 'burgundies', 'port type wine', sherry and Chablis. Wine from the barrels was bottled, corked and labelled in the cellar by hand, in bottles or in flagons or ½ flagons, a flagon being equal to 1½ bottles. A wine described as an 'M & S special burgundy' cost 4/- a flagon, with Emu Burgundy at 4/6d. An additional 3d was charged per flagon, refunded when returned in good condition.

Cider was also bottled from barrels, some in large 4 quart flagons for as little as 3/-, but customers could also buy a quart (2 pints) flagon. One cider was, somewhat surprisingly, recommended for medicinal purposes. Other drinks bottled in Matthew's cellars included Finest Old Jamaica rum at 12/- a bottle. What proportion of wine and spirits sold came already bottled and what proportion was bottled on the premises is not known but the practice of buying in bulk, bottling and labelling continued until the shop closed.

10.3 Bottling and labelling wine imported in large barrels, always part of Matthew's practice, 1913.

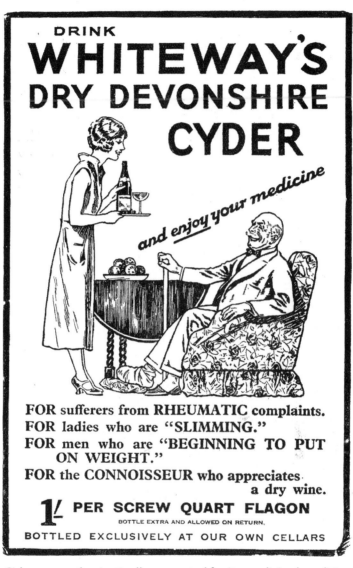

10.4 Cider was enthusiastically promoted for its medicinal qualities, 1936.

The pre-Christmas period was very busy. Richard Matthew, Bernard's older son, worked in the cellar in his school holidays in the mid 1950s, bottling wine straight from the hogshead, then corking and labelling each bottle. Stephen, his younger brother, who helped make up the orders in the cellar in 1959 in his Christmas holidays from school, remembers one of the cellarmen:

Charles Heidsieck

CHAMPAGNE

Vintages 1926 & 1928

Finest Extra Qual., Extra Dry

Specially Recommended

Always the Best —

— For Yourself and Your Guest

Also in Quarter Bottles
Non Vintage, Extra Dry

10.5 Non-vintage champagne was also offered in quarter bottles for 3/9d, 1936.

Bob wore a cap, boots, and ties around the bottom of his trousers. His job was to fill, cork, and label the bottles from the bulk wine that Matthew's imported. 'You name it, we've got it', was his catch cry, as requests for more bottles came down to the cellar from the wine shop.

Some wines were promoted as having been bottled at the chateau from which they came and these superior wines cost around 8/- a bottle in 1936. Bernard Matthew's favourite personal tipple, Tio Pepe, a pale dry sherry, cost 8/6 in 1936 but sherries could go up to 12/6. Customers could purchase many drinks in ½ bottles as well, some even in ¼ bottles, or they could save money by buying in dozens. As well as shipping wine from Australia and from South Africa, Matthew's imported wine from Europe: France, Spain, Germany, Portugal and Hungary. All wines were purchased through the agencies of the actual growers of the wine and shipped direct, so saving middleman's charges. Prices, the firm maintained, would be found to be 'extremely moderate' and customers were urged when comparing costs with other shops to note the quality of their wine:

> We only purchase the best vintages in each district and pass over the years when a vintage is a poor one. We respectfully ask our customers to compare the quality we offer before accepting wines of doubtful origin and seemingly low prices.

Ales and stouts offered in the wine shop were often local. The hoppy smell of Greene King's beer, brewed at their Panton Street brewery in Cambridge, is recalled by Perse School girls whose classrooms were across the road. Matthew's also sold Bailey and Tebbutt's beer made in Cambridge and Tollemache's brewed in Ipswich. Guinness, of course, was from Dublin and Munich beer, 'in reputed pints', came from Germany. Some beer was in firkins – 4½ gallon casks. Matthew's also sold liqueurs, spirits, medicated wine, sacramental wine and sirops and were agents for 'Sparklets', advertised as a new and cheap way of aerating all liquids at home. When a Domestic Exhibition was held at the Corn Exchange in 1899, Matthew's took part with their Sparklets, giving practical demonstrations of this modern gadget.

Customers

Customers of the wine shop included well-off townspeople living in substantial houses with their own wine cellars. Before the First World War two special services were offered, inspection of their cellars at home, and their wines examined. Wines could be re-corked if necessary, this being recommended at the time as good practice every ten years. By the 1930s, recognising that a smaller proportion of their customers had their own cellar, the firm instead offered free storage in Trinity Street, with wine delivered when required:

> We can offer free storage for parcels of wine purchased from us. As modern houses are often without a wine cellar this service is greatly appreciated. Delivery will be made from customers' own stocks in suitable quantities as directed.

Many university Fellows bought their wine from Matthew & Son. Dr Glyn Daniel, archaeologist and Fellow of St John's and well known for his TV programme Animal, Vegetable and Mineral in the 1950s, lived in a flat nearby in St John's Street. He would call in, a member of staff remembering his long scarf wound round his neck, reaching down to the floor, and request, 'A bottle of my usual'. From 1946, for nearly ten years, Glyn Daniel had been Steward at St John's College and no doubt on the mailing list for Matthew's small wine catalogue which they produced for their customers once or twice a year. He recalled when he had served a wine to Colin McIver from Dolamore's, the London wine merchants who advised St John's:

> On one occasion I served blind a Mouton d'Armailacq '47 which I had got from Matthews the grocers in Trinity Street. 'What's this, my boy?', he said, 'It's marvellous.' I told him what it was, that Matthews had twenty dozen, and the price they were offering it to me. 'Buy the lot, he said, 'and if you don't like it in a year's time, Dolamore's will take it from you.' I went nervously to the telephone and bought the lot: a wine that was most appreciated in the college over the next three years.

Two of the firm's travellers, staff visiting customers in their homes or businesses, specialised in wine, often taking regular small orders from Cambridge residents for a selection of fine wines and spirits.

10.6 Wine catalogues were produced regularly for customers.

But sometimes the orders were somewhat larger. Ivan Wallman remembers that one year the butler at Burleigh House, a stately home in Lincolnshire, made an order from Matthew's to use as Christmas presents for staff on the estate. Ivan had called on the off chance – travellers were paid commission and had no limit set on where they could go – and left some samples and a price list with the butler. A few days later he took a phone call in the shop from him for an order for 12 dozen bottles of whisky, as long as it could be delivered to Burleigh by Christmas Eve – which was in two days time. It was taken in a minivan that same day. Other travellers' regular customers included golf clubs and working men's clubs, with vanloads of their orders going out every week as far as Bedford and Hertfordshire.

On occasion Matthew & Son would invite their regular customers to a wine tasting event, one of which indirectly made a small contribution to a huge discovery. James Watson described an episode in the work on the structure of DNA in 1951. Before the final breakthrough, his colleague Francis Crick, working at home, found he had an answer to a problem which proved to be an important step in the discovery. But Crick stopped work on crucial equations to attend a wine tasting with his wife Odile at Matthew & Son, 'one of Cambridge's better wine merchants', as Watson described the shop. Crick was hoping for the company of young women, which he enjoyed, but it was not the evening they had expected:

> For several days his morale had been buoyed by the request to sample the wines. It meant acceptance by a more fashionable and amusing part of Cambridge and allowed him to dismiss the fact that he was not appreciated by a variety of dull and pompous dons. ... To their dismay their companions were college dons contentedly talking about the burdensome administrative problems with which they were so sadly afflicted. They went home early and Francis, unexpectedly sober, thought more about his answer.

The next day saw success: Crick compared notes with colleagues working on the same problem and within a few days a manuscript was jubilantly dispatched to the scientific journal *Nature*, a finding which was of great value in solving the puzzle of DNA two years later.

> To All to Whom these Presents shall come to be read,
>
> *Adolphus William Ward, Litt. D.* and
>
> VICE-CHANCELLOR *of the University of Cambridge,*
>
> *sendeth Greeting.*
>
> ---
>
> KNOW Ye, That I the said VICE-CHANCELLOR, in the name and on the behalf of the CHANCELLOR, MASTERS and SCHOLARS of the said University, have admitted, and by these Presents have allowed *Matthew & Son, Limited, Provision Merchants, Sidney Street* of the Town of Cambridge, to be one of the Vintners of the said University, and by Himself or his Servants, in the house in which he now dwelleth, or on the premises thereunto belonging, situate and being within the said Town and University of Cambridge and the Precincts thereof, to utter, sell, and retail, Foreign Wine of all sorts whatsoever.
>
> In Witness thereof, I have unto these Presents set my Seal of Office, to continue during the good will and pleasure of Me and my Successor. Given at Cambridge this *10th* day of *March* in the year of our Lord *1902*.
>
> *A. W. Ward V.C.*

10.7 *The Vice-chancellor of the University, in 1902 Sir Adolphus William Ward, licensed vintners to sell wine in Cambridge.*

Licensed vintner

The firm was a vintner licensed by the University. In 1382, King Richard II had given the University the right to monitor the quality of wine and beer, and this power was reinforced in 1743 by the Universities (Wine Licences) Act. Oxford's licensing powers were subsequently repealed but Cambridge's lasted until 2003. The Act stated:

'Within the University of Cambridge and the precincts thereof no person shall sell wine by retail unless such person should be duly licensed so to do by the university.' It was originally intended to protect people from poison, maintain order and raise revenue and covered the area five miles around the University.

Customers could not buy alcohol to take away at any time they wanted, for wine shops, as a Matthew's wine list of 1936 mentions, were only allowed to sell over the counter between the hours of 10 a.m. and 2 p.m., and after 6 p.m. However, Matthew & Son offered free delivery for alcohol purchased at any time of the day.

Products for smokers

A third of Matthew & Son's 1936 price list of wines, spirits and tobacco was devoted to products for smokers. In 1948, when surveys of smoking began, smoking was extremely prevalent among men in Britain: 82 per cent smoked some form of tobacco and 65 per cent were cigarette smokers, while 41 per cent of women smoked.

Matthew & Son sold cigarettes, tobacco and cigars. A wide variety of cigars, seen at the time as a sign of authority, wealth and power, were offered, from Cuba and the USA, one being Matthew's own brand, and all promoted in their usual confident way. Cigarettes included Matthew's Special Turkish blend, at 5/- for 100, and two lines that were strongly recommended were Matthew's Special Virginia at 4/10d for 100 and their Special Turkish blend, in cedar boxes for 5/-. More ordinary brands were sold at 6d for ten, Player's Navy Cut and Craven A for example. Cigarettes came from Turkey, Egypt, Russia and the USA. Tobacco was sold by the ounce, 2 oz, ¼ lb and even ½ lb. Prices ranged from 10½d per ounce to 2/1d.

A top quality wine merchant

Matthew's wine shop was one of many in Cambridge. In 1913 and in 1936, the years for which their wine price lists are available, around 26 wine merchants were listed in *Spalding's Street Directory*. But only half were town centre shops and apart from Whitmore & Son of Downing Street, a wine merchant established in 1770 and with a similarly impressive wine list, few shops made wine a substantial part of their business. Matthew & Son was one of the top high class wine merchants in the town, with wine complementing their quality grocery goods. Without this reputation Harvey's, the prestigious Bristol wine merchant, might well not have begun to have shown interest in acquiring Matthew & Son, as they did in the early 1960s.

10.8 Cigars, specially made for Matthew & Son, 1936.

11: WORKING FOR MATTHEW'S

Members of staff at Matthew & Son were well-known for their outstanding personal service to customers. The company's work was very labour intensive, requiring substantial numbers of employees to serve customers but also to undertake many other different tasks as well. Taking and making up orders, delivery, preparing food for sale and packaging it, bottling wine, doing accounts and billing, chasing bad debts and devising promotions and displays: all of this took time. There were few short cuts and many different skills were needed.

Staff memories

Joyce Bailey worked as a cashier for Matthew's, first in The Café and then in the grocery shop, and her husband was a van driver for the bakery:

> I must say they were the happiest days of my life, not a very good wage but we all worked as a team. I was the cashier but had to help with everything from dusting, serving, servicing and sweeping the floor. There were early breakfasts and I used to help before the shop opened. Our bakery was in Green Street and one could leave their cycle all day and still find it there when we left at 7 p.m. We were very busy those days. We didn't have holiday days like they do now. When the war broke out I was transferred to the office in the grocery shop with Mr Williams and he taught me all I know about accounts.

Mr Williams had joined the firm before the First World War, returning from war service with only one arm and rising to be Chief Cashier. Margaret Graves, who joined the staff straight from school in 1955, also a cashier working with Mr Williams, remembered him counting notes faster than she could. Mrs. Graves, née Cage, found Matthew's a very friendly shop to work for and recalls an important event in her life when she was there:

> It had a side entrance off Green Street. On my way back from my dinner hour with my boyfriend, we came through the side way and he asked me to marry him and gave me a Ruby and Diamond ring. The lovely china Department was run by Eddie Haylock, Mrs. Trotter and one of three sisters, [who all worked for the firm]. Just before I married I used to buy china from there, two items a week until the set was complete.

Staff had a discount for their purchases, 10% in some departments and 12½% in others.

The working week

In the mid nineteenth century staff worked long hours in retail shops in Cambridge, with businesses shutting at 9 p.m. in summer and 7 p.m. in winter. By 1871 a local agreement had been reached that shops would shut at four o'clock one afternoon a week in the summer months. And in 1911 The Shops Act was passed, making it obligatory for shops to shut at 1 p.m. one day a week for a staff half day, in Cambridge this being a Thursday. Shops were required to ensure that their assistants were off the premises by 1.30 that day, so Matthew's customers were urged to submit their orders for delivery on Wednesday if possible, or quite early Thursday morning.

In the 1950s, cashiers worked from 9 in the morning until 5.30 p.m. Monday to Saturday. They had a half day on Thursday still, a half day off on a Saturday once a month, and a week's paid holiday. Mr Williams, being Head Cashier, worked each Saturday, unless Cambridge City was playing at home when Margaret Graves went in to cover for him:

> When I left to have my daughter in 1961 I went to work on a Saturday afternoon when Cambridge City were playing at home so Mr Williams could go to the match. Mother in law looked after the baby. My husband and his brother had to go to the football as well so she could have her to herself.

Mrs Graves' wages were £2.5.0 when she started work in the 1950s and her bus fare took 10/-, so in time she bought a new bike and cycled to work instead. She did not contribute to a pension. Friday was Pay Day when staff were paid in cash, lining up to receive their pay in envelopes prepared by the cashiers during the week:

> While working on the cash desk or cashier's office, we used to write all the wage packets out, names only. They were small brown envelopes with holes at the bottom corner so you could count the change and a top corner cut off so you could count the notes without opening the envelope.

Social and sporting activities

In peace time, staff outings, run by the M & S Social Club, were a regular feature of the year for Matthew's employees. In 1909, seventeen male staff members went to Brighton. Great Yarmouth was the destination in 1925, this time with many women staff. In 1947 the first post-war annual outing to Southend was on Thursday July 10th, the day no doubt chosen because it was early-closing, leaving the shop at 7.15 a.m. Boyfriends could come too.

Staff dinners included a reunion dinner and concert after the war, held in The Guildhall in 1946. Ivan Wallman, who worked as a rep in the wine department, enjoyed a Christmas party in the early 1960s for staff and their spouses with dinner and dancing till midnight, held at The Dorothy Café and attended by 200 people. He dressed up for the occasion, 'I wore flared trousers and a jacket with velvet cuffs and collar.' And in December 1964, after the business had been closed down, there was a reunion dinner at the Golden Hind Hotel. A traditional roast meal featured on all the menus. There is no record of any staff dramatic club as there was at Robert Sayle, but there was a music society at one time and there were sporting groups, one being the MFC, Matthew's Football Club, known as 'The Doughnuts.'

Staffing

Early on in the firm's life, it would appear that the owners did much of the bookwork. Matthew & Gent employed seven to eight men but David Matthew and John Gent signed customers' bills. In 1889 John Matthew was still recording provisions bought by the Assize Judge, but then he was a very special customer. By the start of the

11.1 *The Brighton outing was all men, somewhat formally dressed, 1909.*

11.2 Great Yarmouth was the destination for staff on a sunny day. Bernard Matthew is seated, eighth from left, leaning forward, 1925.

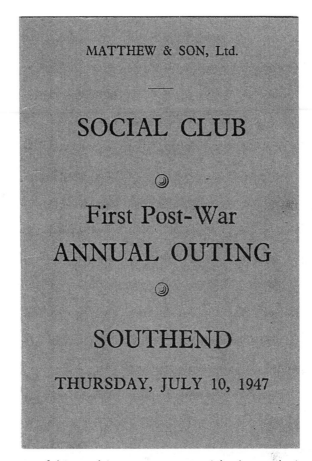

MATTHEW & SON, Ltd.

——

SOCIAL CLUB

First Post-War
ANNUAL OUTING

SOUTHEND

THURSDAY, JULY 10, 1947

11.3 'Take care of this card. It represents your ticket,' were the instructions from the Social Club on the reverse, 1925.

twentieth century, as the business expanded, the number of employees grew substantially. In 1913 a journal article records that Matthew's employed 150 people, though a photo taken in 1909 shows nearer 100, all men, so the exact number is uncertain. In March 1961 a detailed staff record compiled by hand by Bernard Matthew showed that most employees worked full time, but in Order Assembly, where nineteen people were employed and in The Café and its shop with twenty eight members of staff, there were substantial numbers of part-timers. Altogether Matthew & Son had 137 employees in 1961, made up of four departmental managers, ninety three other full-time staff and forty part-timers.

11.4 The post-war reunion dinner, held in a packed Guildhall, December 16th 1946.

11.5 'The Doughnuts', the name adopted by Matthew's Football Club. The captain was P.E. Jordan in 1933.

11.6 *The staff of Matthew & Son, 1909.*

The firm felt they were fair employers. Employees could use the staff canteen, opened in 1947, for their tea breaks morning and afternoon and for a hot meal at lunch time. A report made to the Directors that year showing a post-war recovery in most of the firm's departments commented on the improved quality and spirit among the staff, 'which was also noted by the public'. Wages, however, were seen as a problem for a firm offering such a labour intensive service and in competition with other local employers for staff, and an increase in wages for office staff had to be agreed in 1946:

> Higher wages elsewhere have not been sufficient to draw staff away from the fair rates and conditions they receive as employees of this Company. But it is a daily problem to attempt to balance constantly rising wage costs by improved quality of labour and methods. [The wages increase was] due to the necessity of improving the poor quality of clerk employed during the war and to the extremely high wages obtainable elsewhere by shorthand typists and accounting machine operators.

Salaries for departmental managers of sales sections were worked out half-yearly, on a scale for Shop Managers under the agreement with the Retail Food Trades Wages Council. Mr Stearn the Grocery Manager, for example, who had originally joined the staff at the age of 16 in 1924, received commission according to the volume of sales on top of his salary and was a member of the pension scheme.

Mr Stearn stayed for 38 years in all, apart from war service in World War Two, and was one of a number of very long-serving members of staff. Mr Thomas Peers, who died in 1935, worked at Matthew & Son for over 53 years. 'Billy' Williams, as he was known to older members of staff, stayed for 50 years and was one of five staff members who were honoured at an event in 1963. Four others also received retirement awards for between 40 and 43 years service with the firm, all five together having a total of 216 years with Matthew's. Miss Cissie Barton, head waitress, for 43 years; Miss Olive Pamplin, head of the Order Bureau, for 42 years service; Mr Herbert Sadler, the coffee roaster, for 41; and Miss Ranyard, Manageress of The Café, for 40.

11.7 Bernard Matthew presenting a long-service award to Mr H. Williams after 50 years' service, 1963.

11.8 *Other staff with their awards, l to r, Mr Herbert Sadler, Mr H. Williams, Miss E. Ranyard, Miss Olive Pamplin and Miss Cissie Barton.*

Equipped for the job

Staff became very skilled at their jobs. Margaret Graves remembered the grocery counter:

> Mr Nunn used to weigh out the tea. He would lay a sheet of paper about A4 size on the Counter, tip the tea on to it and fold it to a neat package. How he folded it, it didn't need sticky tape to hold it together and he also ground the coffee and wrapped it in the same way.

Elaborate wedding cakes were produced in the bakery. Window displays and exhibits at exhibitions were meticulously done, many of which won prizes. In 1950, when Annie Get Your Gun was being screened at the Central Cinema, their prize-winning display had the theme 'Doing what comes naturally – when you shop at Matthew & Son'. In 1951 the Display Manager, Mr Walter Bedford, was responsible for the firm winning first prize in a national competition of £250 from Hedley's, the soap manufacturers and in 1953, a £50 prize was awarded for a Ryvita and Squish window display. Ray Gordon and Johnny Warwick worked in the basement to cut and bone the sides of bacon, another skilled job. The Wine Shop Manager, Terence Zarattini, was immensely knowledgeable about its wide range of wines and spirits. Celia Matthew, Bernard's elder daughter, with very little experience of wine drinking, remembers being trained by Mr Terence, as he was known, when she worked in the wine shop in her university vacations in the 1950s. Stephen Matthew, Bernard's younger son, working in the cellars, admired a skill he found he sadly could not imitate:

> I recall the cellar master holding 14 bottles of wine at one time. Imagine four in one hand, squeezed between the fingers and thumb, about seven stacked under the arm from wrist to armpit, and another two or three in the other hand. I tried to emulate his artistry. I dropped a handful of bottles on one occasion.

The high standard expected of Matthew's staff was remembered by many employees. In 1985 Christopher South wrote an article in the local paper reminiscing about Matthew & Son, amazed at the prices charged in 1936, and ended, 'I bet they even smiled at you and said

11.9 A £250 prize comes to Cambridge, Cambridge Daily News, September 13th 1951. Mr A Simpson, a Director of Matthew & Son, is on the right.

11.10 The grocery and provisions section of the shop showing the uniformed staff, 1927.

11.11 The doorman's cap, still to be seen today in the Cambridge Folk Museum.

'Thank you' as you handed them your money.' But Vic Merryweather, a former member of staff, firmly corrected him:

> Never did Matthew's assistants say 'thank you'. It was always 'Thank-you Sir or Thank-you Madam.' One member of staff even said, 'Thank-you Modom'.

But Mrs Graves had a clear recollection of one less than honest member of staff:

> There were three reps who used to go out to customers to collect money and pay it into the cashier's office. One embezzled quite a lot of money so we had to go to court.

Members of staff were expected to look smart and clothing was provided for most employees. A picture of the interior of the Grocery Shop in 1927 shows all staff in white coats, apart from Arthur Chapple,

Departmental Manager, who wore a suit, and the doorman, Arthur French, in a jacket and peaked cap. In greengrocery, staff wore green; in despatch and delivery, brown; and in the bakery, white. White coats with chefs' tall white hats were worn by men and white coats with caps by women.

At that time there was no collection by Securicor, just a member of staff on their bicycle. Mrs Graves wrote:

> I used to collect the day's takings each day from the branch shops and cycle to Cambridge with the money in a carrier bag. One day I had just collected money from the Shelford shop when I was knocked off my bike by a Police Car as they opened the car door. They took me to the doctor's then back home but then I cycled back to Cambridge to Trinity St. The Police did call in the shop to let them know I was on the way. Thankfully I didn't have to cycle to any other branches.

The effects of war

Like all businesses, Matthew & Son was affected in many ways by war. Over the four years of the 1914-18 war, 102 male members of staff enlisted or were called up and their names were recorded in a special long thin brown notebook. Nearly half, forty five men, were re-engaged after the war. Only five men had died on active service, a surprisingly small proportion. All who served were honoured in a full page advertisement published in the *Cambridge News*:

> The Directors of Matthew & Son Ltd desire to thank their Customers for the consideration and indulgence extended to them through the strenuous days of the war. Although they have endeavoured with their depleted staff to give satisfaction, under the difficult conditions, to all orders received. M. & S. hope with the advent [of] PEACE and the return in the near future of some of their old experienced employees to give their patrons the attention of pre-war days.

Among those returning in 1918 was Mr Arthur Adams, who had begun work at Matthew's in 1906 as an errand boy, making deliveries on a bicycle. Later he was in charge of the Despatch Department for many years and became Staff Manager before leaving to start his own business. His son was called Bernard, named after Bernard Matthew.

Bernard Matthew, born in 1900, did not serve in the First World War, though was a member of the Cambridge University Officers' Training Corps in 1918, and at the start of the Second World War he was 39 and served in the Home Guard. Just too old then to be called up, he was designated as being in a reserved occupation as a manager of a business largely concerned with retail food distribution. His elder brother Gordon, CBE, DSO served in the regular army in both World Wars.

Very happy years

From the accounts contributed by members of staff to this history it does seem that Matthew's of Trinity Street was a good place to work. 'They were very happy years,' as Mrs Joy Amis, a member of staff at the Shelford branch, recalled. People stayed with the firm and daughters, sisters and husbands came to join existing members of staff, neither likely to have happened if it had not been so. People working for Matthew & Son remembered it as a good time of their lives.

12: MATTHEW'S CUSTOMERS

When people recall shopping at Matthew & Son they tend to do so with great pleasure, but not just for the wonderful smell of roasting coffee and the courtesy of the staff. For children, when accompanying their parents or grandparents the great excitement of shopping at Matthew's was the overhead cash system. Like many larger shops of the time, for many years Matthew & Son used a cash railway where the cash and a handwritten receipt were placed in a small container. Matthew & Son used the ball system, the earliest type developed. The counter assistant raised the ball, which divided in half and closed securely to prevent anything dropping out, up on to the overhead track in a lift by pulling a cord. After travelling at what seemed to the children to be lightning speed, it arrived at the cashier's desk. The cashier placed the change and the stamped receipt in the ball and returned it to the same counter along the track. 'The children looked up in awe,' recalls Mrs Alice Zeitlyn of Chesterton. The system had been invented in the 1880s in America and was installed in shops all around the world till the 1920s. Matthew's continued to use theirs until the mid twentieth century, when the cash railway gave way to a system where customers went to the cashier's desk to pay for their items and get their change and receipt, and later a till was installed on each counter.

If a customer had an account there would still be a leisurely interval, waiting while coffee was ground, butter was cut in the amount required, bacon was sliced and cheese cut with a wire – all carefully wrapped. Chairs, also fondly remembered, were placed sideways on to each counter and were a welcome service for the waiting shopper.

University customers

Matthew's customers included the University, visitors and local residents. An early university customer was a correspondent of Charles Darwin, Charles Babington, a Fellow of St John's College. A bill

12.1 A line of chairs for customers to use in the Provision department, 1913.

shows items he bought in 1834 from Matthew & Gent over a five month period, at a cost of £2.12.11, (with a 2/5 discount for cash), including groceries and cleaning materials such as a mop for 2/-, soap 8d and [pumice] stone at 2d. There was no electric light, of course, in college rooms and C.C. Babington also bought 6 tapers at 9d and made regular purchases in the winter for a bottle of sperm oil for his lamps, at 1/10 a bottle.

A Student's Guide to the University of Cambridge, published in 1862, set out what students were expected to supply for their rooms: house linens, crockery, glass, some hardware and other items. To avoid spending too much money students could make an arrangement with their bedder, who could supply a second-hand set of crockery at a cheap rate and rent them teapots, or they could buy their own.

J. Pridden Esq bought a range of goods from Matthew & Gent in 1866 for £2/14/0, paying by cheque, with the receipt stamped with a 1d stamp and signed by John Matthew. Matthew & Son later saw the opportunity for sales to new undergraduates and printed a blank two-column order form listing all they might need. In September 1908 W.R. Chawner Esq. of Emmanuel College, an undergraduate from 1908-11, used the form to order a wide range of items for his room,

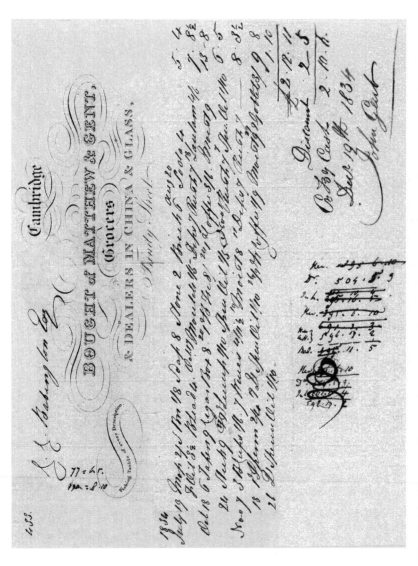

12.2 A bill for C.C. Babington, later to become Professor of Botany, who was known as 'Beetles Babington', 1834.

12.3 Professor Babington became a distinguished botanist, entomologist and archaeologist, date unknown.

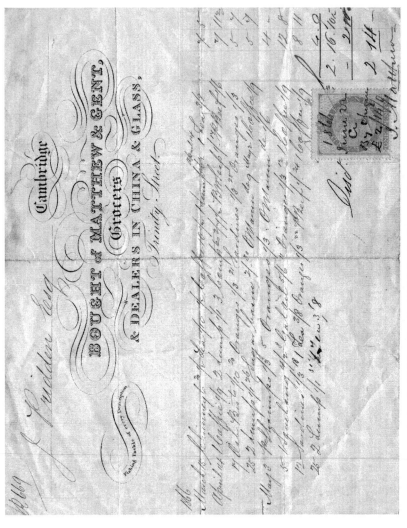

12.4 A bill for purchases made by J. Pridden Esq in 1866, including coffee and tea, oranges, sardines – and a chimney, presumably for a lamp.

W. R. Chawner Esq
J. Emmanuel Colge

To MATTHEW & SON, Ltd.
GENERAL FURNISHERS
China, Glass, Ironmongery, Cutlery, &c.,
GROCERS AND FRUITERERS

The Stores	-	20 & 21	}	Trinity Street,
Wine Dept.	-	19		CAMBRIDGE.
The Cafe -	-	14	}	

Accounts due at the End of the Term.   Five per cent. Discount for Cash.

						Brought forward ...	3	5	8
Breakfast Cups and Saucers						Coal Box			
Tea " "						Fender ...			
Plates ...						Fire Irons			
Egg Cups			1	9		Fire Guard		6	
Cream Jug						Fire Irons			
Slop Basin						Tea Tray			
Sugar "						Waiter ...			
Bread Plate						Kettle ...	8	6	
Milk Jug						Kettle Holder			
Teapot ...			4			Saucepan	3	9	
" Stand			1			Milk ditto			
Hot Water Jug ...						Coffee Pot	5	9	
Luncheon Plates ..			2			Tea Canister	1	1	
2 " Dishes			2	6		Coffee "			
Butter Tub				7		Sugar "			
" Knife						Biscuit "		3	
Bread Trencher ...			1	10		Toast Fork			
" Knife			1	4		Corkscrew	1		
Marmalade Jar ...						Spirit Stove			
Toast Rack						" Kettle			
Cruet Set						Meth. Spirit Can			
Glass Jug (To follow)			1	9		Crumb Brush and Tray			
Salts						Knife Tray			
Salt Spoons ...						Plate Basket			
Tumblers			3	3		Linen "			
Soda Water ditto..						Waste Paper Basket			
Wine Glasses ..						Clothes Brush			
Claret "						Sponge ..			
Decanters						" Basket ...			
Claret Decanter ..						Ale Jug			
Toilet Service			8	6		Ink Stand Ink			
Sponge Drain						Pair Candlesticks			
Toilet Pail			2	11		" Shades and Holders ..			
Bedroom Candlestick						College Match Holder	1		
Bottle and Tumbler			1	6		" Ash Tray			
Lamp ...						" Shields ...			
Shade ...						Hair Broom			
Oil Can						Carpet "			
Filler Cottons						Hearth Brush			
Scissors Bench						Washup Bowl			

12.5 The order form created for new undergraduates by Matthew's, showing purchases made by W.R. Chawner of Emmanuel College in 1908.

spending £4.17.11, though as he paid cash he too received a discount of 4/11. Mr Chawner's purchases included a substantial amount of china and glass and other items, including:

Bread trencher and knife
Toasting fork
Toilet service and pail
Bath can
Kettle
Milk saucepan
Coffee pot
Tea canister
Corkscrew
College match holder
College ash tray
  (both these embossed with Emmanuel College's coat of arms)
Two candlesticks
Two vases

At a later date changes in colleges' buying practices had an adverse effect on some of Matthew's trade. Fewer brushes, for example, were purchased from the 1930s onwards when new systems were adopted by the colleges. They changed their practice to letting fully furnished rooms to undergraduates, with the college supplying one brush of each kind to each bedder, instead of each undergraduate having to buy his own. Bernard had to write a robust reply in 1936 to his cousin Edmund, the Norfolk manufacturer of brushes, who was very indignant about the drop in his orders from Matthew's. Bernard thought this meant the colleges were now buying wholesale for these large orders and had a dig at the colleges:

When you consider there has been this trend in all the other goods we retail in our Hardware Department as well as an increase of the fashion to go to Woolworths, you can understand it has made a great deal of difference. Very few realise the advantages of supporting firms who are tenants of themselves or other colleges. Temptations are put in their way by old members of the college who use their influence with Fellows who have no experience in buying.

The most detailed record of purchases made by individual members of the University can be seen in a heavy ledger kept at Cambridgeshire Archives. It records goods bought from Matthew & Son by undergraduates at nine colleges in the period 1881-6, and by Fellows of Trinity and St John's for the same period. It was not uncommon for Cambridge tradesmen to have to pursue unpaid bills of undergraduates, so they had to give their father's address as well as their college, perhaps a precaution against their bill not being paid at the end of term as required. (Tutors were sometimes also pursued for their students' unpaid bills, though there is no record of this in Matthew & Son's papers.) Montagu Rhodes James, a scholar at King's, gave his father's address as Livermere Rectory, Bury St Edmunds. M.R. James, who became renowned for his ghost stories and his work on early Christianity, later became Provost of King's. While an undergraduate he was a frequent purchaser of tea and of 'siphons', presumably siphons of soda, and among other items bought a teapot, marmalade, mustard and soap. Austen Chamberlain, eldest son of Joseph Chamberlain, the Birmingham politician, later to become a noted politician himself and for five years Chancellor of the Exchequer, was a customer of Matthew's too. He read history at Trinity from 1882-5 and among his purchases were a coffee strainer for 6d and a milk saucepan for 3/6d. No other substantial records of university customers have been found but some bills, one for example made out to Arthur Ernest Taylor who made regular purchases in 1880, are also kept in the Archives.

Married Fellows

Other changes in university practice benefited Matthew's trade. Earlier in the nineteenth century all Fellows were resident in college, but as college rules gradually changed they were no longer required to be celibate and live in. In 1862 Caius was the first college to abolish celibacy, and revised University Statutes finally confirmed this in 1882. Many substantial houses were built in Cambridge around that time, as Fellows married and had children. Seven out of eight houses on a meadow off Madingley Road, for example, were built by Fellows of Colleges. Gwen Raverat, George Darwin's daughter, born in 1885, was described by her biographer as belonging to 'the first hatching of Fellows'. Her father, Fellow of Trinity and Charles

12.6   *A bill for Arthur Ernest Taylor in 1880, when he bought a kettle, a candlestick and an umbrella, as well as groceries.*

Darwin's second son, had married in 1884 and lived in Silver Street. These new households needed a wide range of goods, not just food and drink, but the many items of household equipment which a large house with resident servants would require. Matthew's, with its University connections and offering such a wide choice to its customers was well placed to provide them.

Memories of 20th Century customers

Members of staff remembered many customers of Matthew & Son. Mrs. Bailey wrote:

> We had all the elite in our shop from the Ladies, Enoch Powell, Duke of Devonshire and many more I could name. I remember Anthony Blunt, not knowing then what I know now as being the Spy.

Mrs Graves remembered May Balls in the 1950s:

> A lot of undergrads had accounts at the shop and bought bits and pieces for breakfast. When the May balls were on they came in, in their posh outfits, (the girls had beautiful ball gowns), all bleary eyed and the worse for wear.

Undergraduates bought crumpets for tea, freshly baked in Matthew's bakery. Margaret Marrs, a Girton undergraduate from 1948 to 1951, recalled her tea ration came from Matthew's, but as she mostly had tea in hall she used to take it home:

> My ration of tea would be hardly touched and my mother loved that tea when I went home at vacations. I can still recollect the bags. They were paper, grey and white stripes, with a picture of the outside of the tea shop in orange on one side.

Jean Harvey came to Cambridge in March 1956 and soon found the grocer:

> I remember particularly the way butter was cut from a large lump, and wrapped into the quantities one wanted, and the way coffee was poured on to paper, and a parcel was neatly wrapped and tied with string. I used to buy Bath chaps (pig cheek ham, rolled in breadcrumbs), which made inexpensive and tasty meals to have in my digs. I only remember going to the Café once... it must have been a few months later, when I was meeting a colleague who undertook to tell me how the University worked; I don't remember anything about the meal, but we were married the following year!

Jo Lovegrove shopped in Matthew's in 1956-7, the first year she was married. She loved the shop:

> I remember the lovely bacon we had and I am sure it was cut by the machine. Matthew's delivered all my shopping to Longstanton where we lived. I also remember buying some pretty Poole pottery in pink and blue.

Celebrated Cambridge Visitors

Cambridge was one of the sixty-one Assize towns, visited by judges to try serious court cases. Twice a year Matthew & Gent, as the firm was first known, had an order from the cook of the Assize Judge who came to Cambridge. He had lodgings at the Master's Lodge in Trinity, travelling with his own cook and butler and taking up residence there for a few days each March and July with considerable ceremony. A heavy ledger, donated to the Cambridge Folk Museum by Bernard Matthew, was used to record the Judge's orders – and his prompt payments. A typical order was one made in July 1833, with stationery orders made alongside food and including an extraordinary number of eggs. The order was for:

> Tea, lump [sugar], soap, butter dish (several), mustard, jelly glasses, butter, 60 eggs, pearl barley, lump, 15 lemons, raisins, currants, almonds, York hams, cheese, stilton, 30 eggs, quire foolscap [paper], ball pack thread, bottle capers, 30 eggs, 30 eggs, moist [sugar], lump [sugar], anchovies, reading sauce, salt, vinegar, and moist.

In the twentieth century, other notable visitors patronising the shop included visiting actors at the Arts Theatre. Cyril Fetcher, star of the annual pantomime at The Arts, and Jack Hulbert and his wife Cicely Courtneidge were to be seen buying items in Matthew & Son. In 1958 the film Bachelor of Hearts, about college students and starring Sylvia Sims and Hardy Kruger, was shot in Cambridge. It included scenes on Trinity Street, and the stars came into the shop for a few odd groceries. And in 1960, when the Lord Lieutenant entertained The Queen to lunch in Trinity, Matthew's provided the wines.

Regular customers and rationing

Mr Sills of 'Hillstead', a substantial house in Great Shelford, was one of many customers who were called on weekly for their order, written out in their personal account book. Mr Sills' handsome notebook, with 'Matthew & Son Ltd, The Stores, Cambridge' embossed in gold leaf on the cover, details his orders. From 1913 to 1917 they included a range of fresh goods such as cheese, bacon and lard, tea and coffee, brandy and sherry and household goods such as soap and candles. Mr Sills paid weekly. Matthew's member of staff collected his payment and took his next order.

During rationing in the Second World War, Matthew's had 1,926 households and 5,052 persons registered with them, only able to buy the amount of certain basic items their coupons entitled them to, for

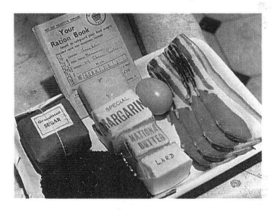

12.7 Rations for one week, 1941-2.

example sugar, tea, margarine, butter, lard, eggs, bacon and cheese. Rationing continued for some goods for a number of years afterwards, tea staying on ration until 1950. Customers were desperate to get some goods not on ration but very scarce, such as tins of salmon, but even Matthew's had problems getting such delicacies. Among those registered were Mrs Enid Matthew from Caxton, Bernard's wife, and Daphne Wyatt from Landbeach, a farmer's wife who worked in Cambridge and, being a town girl originally, preferred the greater anonymity of a town store for her shopping. The weekly delivery service to the outlying villages allowed many country customers without cars to use Matthew's.

'Matthew's for quality, Matthew's for good service'

'Matthew's for quality, Matthew's for good service' was an advertising slogan regularly used by the firm. Cambridge was a prosperous town with a rich university, a town where a shop like Matthew's could expect to attract the custom of better-off residents. Some students and other local people recall the shop but also remember they found it too expensive and shopped elsewhere. There were plenty of other grocers to choose from, over 100 in Cambridge by the early 1960s. But customers of Matthew & Son were prepared to pay that bit more for the quality of the goods and for the quality of personal service offered by the firm.

13: EXPANSION AND GROWTH – AND THE END

OF THE STORY

David Matthew's first small venture on Trinity Street grew to a substantial business over the 130 years the firm was trading. 'The enterprising firm of Messrs Matthew & Son', as a newspaper article in 1896 described it, expanded into much bigger premises, employed a large workforce, developed a network of local branches, and ran a fleet of delivery vans, a bakery and a café. There were some set-backs and contractions, but very few compared to the steady development of the business through most of its life.

Steady expansion

David Matthew, and then his brother John, had largely worked on getting the business established and consolidated. But one important decision for which John was responsible was the move along Trinity Street, about 1858, to numbers 20–21, a much larger building which remained the firm's main shop from then on. These excellent premises were an important reason for Matthew's success: in central Cambridge, on a prestigious street, near large colleges and with the chance to extend both behind and below the original shop.

Two phases of particular growth followed. The first, in Arthur Matthew's time, was from the 1870s to 1917 and the second in his son Bernard's period as Managing Director, from the 1930s to the 1960s. Arthur was responsible for many developments. Between 1884, when Arthur became a partner with his father and 1917, when he died, there were nine periods of substantial new activity.

Business was clearly flourishing during this period, Arthur had flair and ambition and Trinity College was a supportive landlord. The opening of The Café at 14 Trinity Street was a major step but two other developments were also of special significance: the acquisition of Lincolne & Son, and extensive building works undertaken between 1901–1903 and in 1911.

EXPANSION UNDER ARTHUR MATTHEW'S LEADERSHIP

- **1894**   Lease of 19 Trinity Street taken on
- **1895**   Enlargement of cellars
- **1896**   The Café opened in 14 Trinity Street & premises in Green Street taken on
- **1898**   Extensive adaptations of 19–21 Trinity Street
- **1899**   Acquired Lincolne & Son, extending premises and yard
- **1901–3**   New buildings, stables rebuilt & fire hydrant installed in the yard
- **1904**   Improvements to the front of The Café and internal improvements
- **1911**   Further alterations to 19–21 Trinity Street
- **1912**   New despatch warehouse opened in Gifford Place off Green Street

---

Lincolne & Son, also a wine merchant and a Licensed Vintner to the University, was based at 35 Sidney Street, backing on to Matthew's premises. In 1899 an agreement was made between John Lincolne and Matthew & Son to buy Lincolne's leasehold, plant and fixture, book and other debts and cash in hand, as well as goodwill. The sum agreed was £5,892.1.10d, made up of £1,500 cash and the balance in shares of the purchaser's company. John Lincolne became a Director of Matthew & Son at a salary of £400 a year. The lease of 35 Sidney Street included a yard and outbuildings, but there is no record of any trading being carried out in Lincolne's former shop. The value of the purchase was in acquiring more space in the yard and improved access to the site from Sidney Street, as well as integrating a competitor. It was the first of a number of take-overs of other businesses by Matthew's.

13.1 The impressive frontage of the shop at 19 –21 Trinity Street after major alterations, 1913.

Trinity College, as their landlord, helped with extensive alterations to the premises, particularly in the work carried out in the period 1901–3 and again in 1911. Both sets of alterations were complex plans, involving several businesses, not just Matthew & Son's, and requiring constant liaison between them all. From the extensive correspondence and the length of time taken, it clearly was not an easy task to expand premises on a cramped town centre site, and the architects involved did not always agree. But Arthur appreciated the College's support, writing to the Senior Bursar in 1903 to thank Trinity:

> We are very much obliged to the College for the liberal manner in which they have helped us over the extra work and in the Architect's fees. We also sincerely thank you for the consideration received at your hands throughout this somewhat troublesome undertaking.

At one point in 1911, when Arthur and his architect proposed a change of plan, Trinity's architect wrote to the Senior Bursar in exasperation, 'Matthew's are odd people.' The alterations had clearly again been a 'troublesome undertaking' but in the end cordial relations between landlord and tenant were maintained. It was clear that Trinity College encouraged expansion of the grocery business and improvement of properties the College owned.

Owners not tenants

After the First World War, Matthew & Son took another major step by buying property. In 1919 the firm purchased 14 Trinity Street and The Green Street Rooms. The premises were already in use for The Café and the bakery, leased from the Foster family, owners of the former bank on the site. The terms were £6,500 cash down and a £10,000 bank mortgage, secured from Lloyds Bank Limited. Arthur had died in 1917 but the Directors, especially Maude Matthew their Chairman and Fred Cross acting as Governing Director, continued his entrepreneurial approach. The business must have emerged from the war in a healthy financial state to take such a big step. But this was the only time the firm owned any premises, unlike other Cambridge shops such as Eaden Lilley. Perhaps if they had invested in buying property rather than leasing, the history of the company might have been different, for rising rents were one of the difficulties Matthew's later had to face.

Continued expansion

In the second period of expansion of the firm, between the 1920s and 1950s, Fred Cross and then Bernard Matthew also enlarged the business through more building improvements, including extending the area used for customers of The Café.

EXPANSION FROM THE 1920s TO THE 1950s

- 1921   Structural work in The Café
- 1922   Xmas Shopping Centre introduced in the grocery shop
- 1927   China department & wine cellars enlarged
- 1927   Two upper storeys of The Café opened
- 1929   Simpson & Co., 105 Cherry Hinton Road acquired
- 1937   Wine shop at 249 Chesterton Rd acquired
- 1947   Flack & Judge, 21 St Andrew's Street and 59 Hills Road acquired
- 1950   Horace Reed, 66, High Street, Great Shelford acquired
- 1950s   Grocery and wine shop opened at 40 – 44 Newnham Road

---

The Trinity Street shop continued to expand – an 'Xmas Shopping Centre' for seasonal gifts was launched in 1922 for example – but the firm also took a strategic step by purchasing other businesses, so creating a network of Matthew's branches in other parts of the town.

In 1929, Simpson & Co. at 105 Cherry Hinton Road had been a dwindling grocery business, losing money, with 19 employees and 30 wholesale and 320 retail customers. Mr Simpson had poor health and Matthew & Son purchased the business for £3,411, the purchase price including a very small amount of goodwill. By the following year Fred Cross had halved the loss and was expecting that the following year the accounts would show a profit. The premises later proved to be of great use when the bakery moved from Green Street to the Cherry Hinton site, operating behind the shop.

Purchases of other businesses continued again after the Second World War. Flack & Judge was a flourishing city centre business, a 'High Class Grocers, Provision Merchants and Italian Warehousemen', which had been established at 21 St Andrew's Street since 1894, though there had been a grocery shop there for several centuries. Matthew's bought Flack & Judge in 1947. Seven full-time and two part-time staff were employed and a shop at 59 Hills Road was also included in the sale. The new John Lewis store was built partly on the site of the St. Andrew's Street shop. In 1950 Mr Horace Reed's Central Stores in Great Shelford became a branch of Matthew's with the announcement:

> It will be the aim to continue the high standard of service maintained by our predecessor and we shall offer all customers, old and new, MATTHEW SERVICE and MATTHEW VALUE.

By the end of the 1950s, as well as the central premises on Trinity Street, Matthew & Son were trading in six branches in different parts of Cambridge: St Andrew's Street, Hills Road, Newnham, Shelford, Cherry Hinton and Chesterton, the latter being just a wine shop.

Anxieties and retractions

There were also some retractions in this period and worried discussion on future alternatives. Ownership of The Café was not to last. Perhaps capital was needed by the firm, for in 1938, just 20 years after their purchase, 14 Trinity Street and 14–18 Green Street were sold to Trinity College for £16,250. As part of the deal Matthew & Son, already tenants of Trinity, agreed a 21-year lease of the premises at a rent of £525 per annum. Bernard Matthew tried to persuade the Senior Bursar of the College to prohibit any new tenants in the street from undertaking sales of grocery, wine, spirits or beer. This was however refused.

There was anxiety about the future of the firm at times. Notes in Bernard's handwriting, frustratingly undated, indicate that a number of different options were explored at one time by the Board of Directors. Some quite radical changes were discussed, one that 19–21 Trinity Street should be closed but part of the premises of The Café should be used for grocery sales; another that the Café business could be put

146

on the market; or the bakery business could be sold. None of these ideas materialised. Later on, two branches closed in 1960 when the lease of 59 Hills Road was assigned to a shop called Community Veg and the Shelford shop was closed down after Matthew & Son owning it for only ten years.

1962 – and the decision to sell

1962 was the last year of Matthew & Son as a family owned firm. There was no one single reason for its sale. As the Board reviewed their options, looming substantial rent rises and significant competition had to be taken into account. Sainsbury's, the Co-operative Society and other independent grocers in Cambridge were giving customers cheaper alternatives to a high-class grocer offering personal service, free delivery but higher prices. Supermarkets were opening in other parts of the country and were likely to open in Cambridge. Car ownership was increasing. By 1961, three out of ten households had use of a car, compared with one in fifty in the 1930s, meaning fewer people by then relied on grocery purchases being brought to the door.

Aware of all these trends, by 1960 the Directors were giving serious consideration to the future of Matthew & Son, with some of the Directors being particularly keen to sell their shares and so release their investment. Such a step was not unusual. Research into life cycles of family firms indicates that three generations – Matthew's lifespan – is a common period for a company to flourish if relying on leadership by successive family members. None of us in the next generation had developed an interest in taking over and by 1960 our careers, with encouragement and support from our parents, were going in other directions while our cousins were not yet of an age to be involved.

The Harvey's takeover – a positive step at the time

When a proposal came from a firm of prestigious wine merchants for a subsidiary company of theirs to take over the firm as a going concern, it felt a timely offer. Matthew & Son was sold to John Harvey & Sons, long-established wine merchants in both Bristol and London, in 1962. The well-known Matthew name would be kept and jobs would be preserved. In March 1962 Bernard wrote to all members of staff to tell them the business had been sold to A.J. Smith & Co. Ltd, a subsidiary of Harvey's. The three sections of the business – wine, grocery and the restaurant – would continue and Bernard would remain as Chairman and Managing Director.

At the time, it was a good outcome all round. Staff kept their jobs. Arrangements for the family were acceptable. Harvey's was happy about their purchase, with their Managing Director writing to Bernard Matthew towards the end of 1962, saying how pleased they were with the results to date and congratulating him. And customers could continue to shop at 'Matthew's', with the *Cambridge Daily News* voicing its pleasure on the retention of the name:

> There is a venerable Cambridge story about a Trinity man who wrote to a Selwyn man addressing his letter 'Selwyn College, near Cambridge': the Selwyn man sent his reply to 'Trinity College, opposite Matthew's, the grocers.' This celebrated institution for the consumption of good victuals, licensed and unlicensed, on or off the premises has long had a reputation for good fare. Matthew's may not be contemporary with Trinity but its courtly manners compare very favourably with those of the establishment across the road. Now a firm of wine merchants has taken over the business. Happily the name is to be retained. The old story would not be the same if it had to end 'opposite Smith's, the grocers'.

But in the end …

This apparently satisfactory state of affairs was not to continue. Sadly, the initial promise of the sale to Harvey's did not materialise and in 1964 the shop and its other grocery outlets closed, only two years after the business had been purchased. Matthew & Son was not the only firm of their type to sell to other companies and then close around this time. Burton's, for example, a family grocery business in Nottingham sold out to the Canadian chain Fine Fare in the 1960s and then closed in 1983. Grimbly Hughes in Oxford, a firm whose history mirrored Matthew & Son's, sold to Jacksons of Piccadilly in 1959 but was closed down in 1963.

In Cambridge, Matthew's Café became The Turk's Head Restaurant; Matthew's wine shops became Victoria Wines; and in May 1964

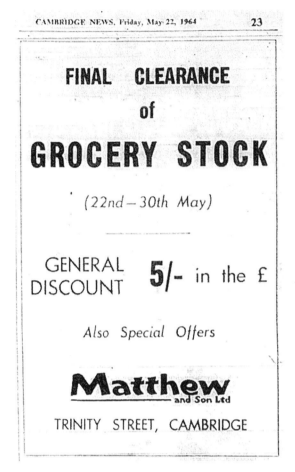

CAMBRIDGE NEWS, Friday, May 22, 1964   23

FINAL CLEARANCE
of
GROCERY STOCK

(22nd – 30th May)

GENERAL DISCOUNT **5/-** in the £

Also Special Offers

Matthew and Son Ltd

TRINITY STREET, CAMBRIDGE

13.2 The final closing sale advertised in the Cambridge Daily News, May 22nd 1964.

the grocery shop was closed by Harvey's, with 45 redundancies. An advertisement placed on May 22nd 1964 confirmed the final closure of Matthew & Son. A compensation scheme was introduced and through liaison with other Cambridge employers, attempts were made to help staff find new jobs, while some employees set up in business by themselves. Bernard Matthew, announcing the closure said:

> One cannot offer a traditional grocery service from a large city centre site at present day rental values. Rather than lower our standards of personal service we have decided to close the department.

Closure but not tragedy

The closure was sad, but it was not a tragedy. The decision to end family ownership had been taken at a time when it was unlikely that the personal service and traditions of Matthew & Son as an independent family firm could continue alone. Rather than going into a decline, selling the business to Harvey's had appeared to be a good opportunity for it to become part of a flourishing larger company. It had been worth trying this option, even if it was not to be successful in the end.

The Matthew family accomplished a great deal in 130 years of trading: they established and expanded a useful business, important to both the university and to residents of Cambridge and Cambridgeshire; the firm was a significant and well-regarded employer; and its leaders played important roles in civic and community life. Let it be so remembered.

ACKNOWLEDGEMENTS

I would like to record my grateful thanks for support and information from a large number of organisations and individuals, particularly to the following:

Cambridgeshire Collection, Cambridge Central Library
Cambridgeshire Archives
The Cambridge & County Folk Museum
Mike Petty
Clare College Archives
Trinity College Archives
Colin Lattimore
The Cambridge News

I also acquired information and received immense encouragement and help from my family, my husband Dick Wilson, my daughter Clare Wilson, my son Jon Wilson, my sister Celia Smith, my brothers, Richard Matthew and Stephen Matthew and my cousin Michael Matthew. Thank you.

I was sustained and inspired by my membership of two writing groups: the writers' workshop of U3AC, The University of the Third Age in Cambridge, and the Lifelines writing group. Thank you to all their members and particularly U3AC tutor Elizabeth Bray and Lifelines members Barbara Roberts and Liz Haggard.

Each time I gave a talk to a local history group I gained more information. U3AC members and Cambridge residents contributed their memories after requests made through the U3AC newsletter and by Mike Petty in his column in the *Cambridge News*. Matthew & Son's 1913 catalogue was returned to me by Colin Lattimore, which my father had given to him and which he too had treasured. I would like to thank them all most warmly.

Keith Smith and Steve Temple used their photographic skills to improve the quality of many of the pictures, Celia Smith produced the family tree from research done by Richard Matthew and Jane Bulleid did a fine job on editing the manuscript. Jon Wilson designed the website *www.cambridgegrocer.com*. All this expertise of family and friends has been very much appreciated. And to David Cronin, of Moyhill Graphic Design, I am most grateful for undertaking the design and doing the back-room work that has made this publication finally possible, and for his skills and knowledge of the challenges of self publishing.

I would also like to thank many other people who contributed memories and helpful information, for which I am most grateful, including Joy Amis, Joyce Bailey, Brenda Bass, Michelle Bullivant, Craig Cressford, Stephanie Dalley, Robin Dyson, Margaret Graves, Jean Harvey, Sheila Jolley, Jo Lovegrove, Margaret Marrs, Catherine Sharp, Eva Shaw, Pat Silk, Ann Silver, St John's College archives, Ann Spokes-Symonds, Polly Stanton, Ivan Wallman, Twigs Way, Eleanor Whitehead, Ann Whitmore, Daphne Wyatt, Megan Zadik, Alice Zeitlyn.

I am deeply grateful to everyone who helped me but the memories of customers and staff became an especially important element in the book. I gained huge amounts of information and insight from a wide variety of individuals and from Cambridge libraries and archives, whose staff, too, were enormously helpful. The story could not have been told if I had had to rely on the limited resources of family memories and our relatively small collection of records and pictures.

Use of published material

I acknowledge the kind permission to use material as follows:
On page iii the map of King's Parade and Trinity Street is from Marcus Askwith, Kevin Taylor, *Central Cambridge. A Guide to the University and Colleges* 1st edition, © Cambridge University Press 1994, reproduced with permission.
Chapter 10: The quotation about the purchase of wine for St John's College is from *Some Small Harvest: The Memoirs of Glyn Daniel* © 1986 Glyn Daniel, reprinted by permission of Thames & Hudson Ltd., London.

The quotation about Francis Crick's attendance at Matthew & Son's wine tasting is reprinted from *The Double Helix* by James D Watson by permission of Weidenfeld and Nicholson, an imprint of The Orion Publishing Group, London © 1968 James D Watson.

Chapter 11: The record of Matthew & Son's employees' war service in the First World War is included by permission of the Roll of Honour *www.roll-of-honour.com.*

I was grateful for information about the cash railway system by Andrew Buxton, whose website is a mine of information about these systems, with links to museums where they have been installed *http://www. ids.u-net.com/cash/*

Chapter 13: The correspondence about renovation in this chapter and elsewhere is included by permission of the Master and Fellows of Trinity College.

Pictures

Many of the pictures in this book come from our family archive but I also acknowledge permission to use illustrations from the following bodies and individuals:

Cambridgeshire Collection, Cambridge Central Library (1.5, 3.3, 3.4, 7.3, 7.5, 7.8, 10.4, 10.6, 10.8)

Cambridgeshire Archives (1.3, 6.8, 7.2, 10.5, 11.6, 11.7, 11.8, 12.3, 12.4)

Cambridge & County Folk Museum (Cover, 11.11)

Mrs M. Graves (6.9)

Cambridge University Library (1.4)

Imperial War Museum image D7958 (12.7)

Note

Thorough attempts were made to find the owner of the copyright for the letter from *The Sunday Times* written in 1950 by W. Arnold Middlebrook, quoted in Chapter 5, but without success. The author is happy to be contacted by anyone who feels their copyright has been infringed.

BIBLIOGRAPHY

Anon *A Student's Guide to the University of Cambridge*, Deighton 1862

Jane Brown and Audrey Osborne, 'Nineteenth-Century Detached Leisure Gardens', *Garden History* 31:1

Olivia Daly *A history of Robert Sayle 1840 – 2007*, John Lewis 2008

Bernard Matthew *Bernard John Matthew 1900–1989 Memoirs, written about 1987*, edited by Celia Smith 2001

Ian Ormes *Eaden Lilley: 250 years of retailing*, W Eaden Lilley & Co Ltd 2000

Sara Payne *Down your street, Cambridge Past and Present*, Vol 1 Central Cambridge, Pevensey Press 1963

Mike Petty *Vanishing Cambridgeshire*, Breedon 2006

Mike Petty, Sarah Woodall and Colin Inman *Cambridge: memories of times past*, Worth Press 2007

Enid Porter *Victorian Cambridge: Josiah Chater's Diaries, 1844–1884*, Phillimore & Co Ltd 1975

Gwen Raverat *Period Piece*, Faber 1952

F.A. Reeve *Cambridge*, Batsford 1976

Frances Spalding *Gwen Raverat: friends, family and affections*, Harvill Press 2001

Frank Stubbings *Bedders, Bulldogs and Bedells: a Cambridge Glossary*, Cambridge University Press 1995

Joshua Taylor Ltd *The Joshua Taylor Story 1810–1960*, Joshua Taylor Ltd 1960

Eleanor Whitehead *A Ramble about New Impington*, Histon and Impington Village Society 1995

John Van Whye *Darwin in Cambridge*, Christ's College 2009

END PIECE:

REFLECTIONS ON WRITING THIS BOOK

After a long absence, in 2004 I returned to live in Cambridgeshire again and coming back revived my interest in the history of the family firm. Bernard Matthew, my father, was its last Managing Director and I had known it all my childhood. The family, of course, shopped there, we would have lunch in The Café and later, in my school holidays, I had worked in one of the branch shops. But I knew little of its history.

My interest became research, for personal memories were not enough when I was invited to speak about the firm at the Histon and Impington Village Society, the local history group in the village near Cambridge where I now live. As I gave talks to other history groups and undertook absorbing visits to libraries and archives, I discovered much more than I had known before. I learnt about the challenge of succession in family firms, not just Matthew & Son; I saw how much my family had contributed to civic and community life in Cambridge; and I realised how moving from living above the shop to their substantial houses was linked to the expansion of their flourishing business at a time of growing prosperity. All these became themes in this book.

I also found out the extent to which the firm was warmly remembered by Cambridge residents and former students and how much interest there was in its history. *Cambridge Grocer* stems from personal interest rather than being an academic study, perhaps not as objective an account as an outsider might have written. But the story of Matthew & Son, the firm and the family, is also a story of Cambridge life, of both its town and its university. The book is more than just a family memoir or an account of one of Cambridge's retail shops. It is a contribution to the social history of Victorian, Edwardian and mid-twentieth century Cambridge and how people lived here. I hope you have enjoyed reading it as much as I enjoyed researching and writing it.

Judy Wilson
July 2010